The ADHD Workbook for Parents

A Guide for Parents of Children Ages 2-12
with Attention-Deficit/Hyperactivity Disorder

Harvey C. Parker, Ph.D.

Specialty Press, Inc.
Plantation, Florida

Specialty Press, Inc.
300 Northwest 70th Avenue, Suite 102
Plantation, Florida 33317
(954) 792-8100 • (800) 233-9273

Printed in the United States of America

ISBN 1-886941-62-9

Library of Congress Cataloging-in-Publication Data

To Roberta, Julia, Michelle and Simon

Table of Contents

Chapter 1   What is ADHD?

A June 2005 report released by the Center for Disease Control indicated that about five percent of children in the United States suffer from difficulties with emotions, concentration, behavior, and getting along with others. These children and their parents and caregivers are often upset and distressed by these difficulties and require support and services. Children with Attention-Deficit/Hyperactivity Disorder (ADHD) make up a significant proportion of this group.

Hardly a day goes by that there isn't an article published in a local newspaper, national magazine, or on the Internet about ADHD. Television talk show hosts have addressed the topic and professional journals and texts in psychology and medicine contain numerous research papers on this disorder. Parent support groups have been forming since the mid-1980's throughout the world to assist families of inattentive and hyperactive children and provide a forum by which parents could exchange information and experiences about raising a child affected by ADHD. In the past ten years, interest in ADHD in adulthood has skyrocketed as we have become aware that this is not just a childhood disorder, but one that can significantly impact the lives of adults as well.

Some of the fervor about ADHD has to do with the medication controversy surrounding the treatment of ADHD. Perhaps interest in the disorder is being generated by parents advocating on behalf of their children to ensure their rights to quality education. Perhaps more attention is being paid to ADHD because we've come to realize that it has very important long-range consequences as we learn that it can have a serious impact on the educational achievement, career attainment, mental health, and overall quality of life of sufferers. No matter the reason for all this interest, it can only do some good. It's hard enough to raise children these days, let alone children with ADHD. Both the parents of children with ADHD, and the children themselves, need help.

Most parents of children with ADHD feel alone. As awareness of ADHD grew, parents found information and support in books, articles, and on the Internet. They realized that the problems they and their child experienced were not unique. Mothers, in particular, and especially mothers of young children with ADHD who are hyperactive and impulsive, frequently feel estranged from other parents. Feelings of parental self-doubt, despondency, and loneliness can easily develop. When these parents meet other parents of children with ADHD, an immediate bond is formed by virtue of a common understanding. The loneliness begins to lessen. Many of these parents describe very similar experiences.

"Whenever we go out to a restaurant, my husband and I spend most of our time reminding Jessica to sit still. She's just impossible to take anywhere. She's always going ninety miles an hour."

"Robert just got his license to drive eight months ago and already he's gotten two tickets and was involved in one accident. He's always in a rush and doesn't seem to think things out before acting."

"I never know what to expect when I pick Steven up at school. I can't believe he's only four and already, everyday he gets a bad report from the teacher. I feel like it's my fault. Just once I'd like to pick him up and see his teacher smiling at me."

"My husband and I can't understand it. We fought with Allison all night to do her homework. First, she didn't remember what to do for homework. Then, when we figured out what the assignment was, she didn't know how to do it. After a two-hour struggle, we finally got it finished. Then, to top it off, this afternoon we got a call from her teacher who told us that she didn't hand it in."

Most parents take their children's behavior for granted. When they go to a movie, parents generally anticipate that their children will watch intently, perhaps asking once in a while for a refreshment. On shopping trips most children tag along with their parents, perhaps occasionally getting impatient and out of hand. When most parents go to open school night they are generally looking forward to seeing their child's classroom and are optimistic that they'll be warmly greeted with a good report from teachers. While such positive experiences are commonplace for most parents, they are often quite uncommon for parents of children with ADHD. Such children, due to their inherent restlessness, excitability, over-exuberance, impatience, and inattentiveness, can turn the most routine family or school day into a problematic situation. Parents frequently blame themselves for their child's problems and often try countless different ways to help their child make a better adjustment.

ADHD is a neurobiological disorder that affects between five and seven percent of the population of children and adolescents and between one and three percent of adults. It is characterized by attention skills that are developmentally inappropriate, and, in some cases, impulsivity and hyperactivity.

Symptoms typically appear in early childhood, although some children develop ADHD later as a result of brain injury from illness or injury. Symptoms may persist into adulthood and can pose life-long challenges. The official diagnostic criteria state that symptoms must occur before age seven, however, there is disagreement among researchers, some arguing that the onset criteria should be broadened to include anytime during childhood.

Early ADHD researchers were primarily concerned with the symptoms of hyperactivity and impulsivity and gave little notice to inattention as a problem. Researchers in the 1980's realized that many children had serious problems paying attention, but had no problems with hyperactivity or impulsivity. We have come to accept that although inattention may not be as noticeable as hyperactivity or impulsivity, it often causes serious problems for the child.

The name of the disorder has changed several times over the past thirty years, each change reflecting advances in our understanding of this complicated condition. The *Diagnostic and Statistical Manual of Mental Disorders: Fourth Edition-TR* (DSM-IV-TR) lists Attention-Deficit/Hyperactivity Disorder as the official name and specifies three types:
- *Predominantly Inattentive Type* for someone with serious inattention problems, but not much problem with hyperactivity/impulsive symptoms;
- *Combined Type* for someone with serious inattention problems and serious problems with hyperactivity and impulsivity; and,
- *Predominantly Hyperactive/Impulsive Type* for someone with serious problems with hyperactivity/impulsivity, but not much problem with inattention.

While the term ADHD is the technically correct term for either of the three types indicated above, in the past the term attention deficit disorder (ADD) was used, and still is by many. For nearly 20 years ADD and ADHD have been used synonymously in publications and in public policy. In this book we will use the term ADHD.

According to the DSM-IV, for a person to have a diagnosis he must often or very often exhibit at least six of the symptoms listed below reflecting either inattention or hyperactivity and impulsivity for at least six months to a degree that is maladaptive and inconsistent with developmental level. These symptoms must have begun prior to age seven, must be evident in two or more settings (home, school, work, community), must impair functioning, and must not be due to any other mental disorder such as a mood disorder, anxiety, learning disability, pervasive developmental disorder, etc.

Inattention Symptoms
- a. often fails to give close attention to details or makes careless mistakes in schoolwork, work, or other activities
- b. often has difficulty sustaining attention in tasks or play activities
- c. often does not seem to listen when spoken to directly

    d.   often does not follow through on instructions and fails to finish schoolwork, chores, or duties in the workplace (not due to oppositional behavior or failure to understand instructions)

    e.   often has difficulty organizing tasks and activities

    f.   often avoids, dislikes, or is reluctant to engage in tasks that require sustained mental effort (such as schoolwork or homework)

    g.   often loses things necessary for tasks or activities (e.g., toys, school assignments, pencils, books, or tools)

    h.   is often easily distracted by extraneous stimuli

    i.   is often forgetful in daily activities

Hyperactive Symptoms

    j.   often fidgets with hands or feet or squirms in seat

    k.   often leaves seat in classroom or in other situations in which remaining seated is expected

    l.   often runs about or climbs excessively in situations in which it is inappropriate (in adolescents or adults, may be limited to subjective feelings of restlessness)

    m.   often has difficulty playing or engaging in leisure activities quietly

    n.   is often "on the go" or often acts as if "driven by a motor"

    o.   often talks excessively

Impulsive Symptoms

    p.   often blurts out answers before questions have been completed

    q.   often has difficulty awaiting his or her turn

    r.   often interrupts or intrudes on others (e.g., butts into conversations or games)

Complete This ADHD Symptom Checklist

Below is a checklist containing the eighteen symptoms of ADHD. Items 1-9 describe characteristics of inattention. Items 10-15 describe characteristics of hyperactivity. Items 16-18 describe characteristics of impulsivity. In the space before each statement, put the number that best describes your child's behavior (0=never or rarely; 1 = sometimes; 2 = often; 3 = very often).

Inattention Symptoms

____   1. Fails to give close attention to details or makes careless mistakes in schoolwork, work, or other activities.

____   2. Has difficulty sustaining attention in tasks or play activities.

____   3. Does not seem to listen when spoken to directly.

____   4. Does not follow through on instructions and fails to finish schoolwork, chores, or duties in the workplace (not due to oppositional behavior or failure to understand instructions).

____ 5. Has difficulty organizing tasks and activities.

____ 6. Avoids, dislikes, or is reluctant to engage in tasks that require sustained mental effort (such as schoolwork or homework).

____ 7. Loses things necessary for tasks or activities (e.g., toys, school assignments, pencils, books, or tools).

____ 8. Is easily distracted by extraneous stimuli.

____ 9. Is often forgetful in daily activities.

Hyperactive-Impulsive Symptoms

____ 10. Fidgets with hands or feet or squirms in seat.

____ 11. Leaves seat in classroom or in other situations in which remaining seated is expected.

____ 12. Runs about or climbs excessively in situations in which it is inappropriate (in adolescents or adults, may be limited to subjective feelings of restlessness).

____ 13. Has difficulty playing or engaging in leisure activities quietly.

____ 14. Is "on the go" or often acts as if "driven by a motor."

____ 15. Talks excessively.

____ 16. Blurts out answers before questions have been completed.

____ 17. Has difficulty awaiting his or her turn.

____ 18. Interrupts or intrudes on others (e.g., butts into conversations or games).

Count the number of items in each group (inattention items 1-9 and hyperactivity-impulsivity items 10-18) you marked "2" or "3." If six or more items are marked "2" or "3" in each group this could indicate serious problems in the groups marked.

How the Types of ADHD Compare

Within the general population, children with the inattentive type outnumber those with the combined type or the hyperactive-impulsive type. However, children with the combined type are more commonly referred to clinics for treatment of ADHD over the other two types. Children with the combined type of ADHD are more likely to have problems with behavior than children with the inattentive type. Those in the combined type are at greater risk for associated problems like oppositional defiant disorder, conduct disorder, tics, and bipolar disorder. These are called co-occurring or co-morbid conditions. They will be discussed in more detail in the next chapter.

Children with the inattentive type are often described as daydreamy or "in a fog." They frequently need reminders to stay focused on a task to completion. They may be under-active rather than over-active and they are often sluggish and complete tasks after others. Even motor activities that don't require a great deal of concentration, like getting ready in the morning, picking up their room, or taking the garbage out, may take longer to complete than average. Because they are sluggish and excessively daydreamy, these children may miss out on learning activities and opportunities to interact. They may be more reluctant to initiate social contact, and they may be more passive than others. They tend to make a greater number of errors on academic tasks or tasks that require sustained concentration because they have difficulty staying focused and outputting a consistent amount of energy to complete the task.

Children in either of the ADHD types show more impairment than children without ADHD on measures of intellectual functioning and academic achievement and are at greater risk for problems in school. Those with the combined type are also more likely to be put into special education classes.

As compared to children who are inattentive alone, those in the combined group tend to be identified earlier because of their behavioral and social problems resulting from impulsivity and poor self-control. Problems with self-control are more easily noticed at younger ages than problems with inattention. Even at age two children who are very hyperactive, impulsive, demanding, and fussy stand out. Children who are quiet and passive don't. Young children are not required to pay attention for long when they are in preschool or in the primary grades. Often it isn't until fourth or fifth grade that more seatwork is given requiring the child to complete work that takes considerable attention and time. While teachers of primary age children may be concerned about the inattentive child who is having trouble completing work or learning, they may not consider the problem to be serious until the child goes on to fourth or fifth grade.

The ADHD research is almost exclusively on children with the combined type. We don't know very much about treatment of children with the inattentive type. We know that all three types respond to ADHD medications. This improves attention and has additional benefits with regard to behavior, eye-hand coordination, and short-term memory. Approximately ninety percent of ADHD children with either combined or hyperactive-impulsive type will have a positive response to stimulants. Fewer of the inattentive children have such a robust positive response. When they do, they may be able to benefit from lower doses of medication than those who are hyperactive and impulsive. The most important issue affecting treatment of children who have different types of ADHD is the presence of associated disorders. For example, disruptive behavior in the form of opposition, defiance, and rule breaking occurs more frequently in children who exhibit signs of hyperactivity and impulsivity as opposed to inattention alone. Problems related to associated disorders will be more fully discussed in the following chapter.

What About Girls with ADHD?

The vast majority of research done in the area of ADHD has been done on boys with very few girls included. In 1999, psychiatrist Joseph Biederman and his colleagues from Massachusetts General Hospital studied a large group girls between ages six and eighteen with and without ADHD and compared the two groups. Of the girls who had a diagnosis of ADHD, fifty-nine percent had the combined type, twenty-seven percent had the inattentive type, and seven percent had the hyperactive-impulsive type. Girls in the ADHD group were more likely to have problems with conduct, mood, anxiety, and substance use than those in the non-ADHD group. Although the girls with ADHD did exhibit disruptive behavior disorders, the frequency was about half as compared to boys with ADHD. However, the rate of mood and anxiety disorders in the ADHD girls group was about equal to that found in boys with ADHD. There was an indication that problems with substance use were more common among girls with ADHD than had been previously found to be true for boys. For example, girls with ADHD were about four times as likely to be smokers. In comparing cognitive skills and academic performance of girls with ADHD and those without ADHD, the ADHD girls were about 2.5 times more likely to be diagnosed with a learning disability, more than sixteen times more likely to have repeated a grade in school, and almost ten times as likely to have been placed in a special class at school.

Psychologist Stephen Hinshaw and his colleagues studied girls with ADHD who were attending a summer treatment program at the University of California, Berkeley and found that compared to a matched control group of non-ADHD girls, they were very impaired academically and socially. Another psychologist, Kathleen Nadeau, has written extensively about ADHD in girls as has Ellen Littman and developmental pediatrican, Patricia Quinn. Their book, *Understanding Girls with ADHD,* is an excellent resource.

The lesson to be learned from these studies is that ADHD is a serious problem in girls just as it is in boys. Clinicians should be aware of ADHD symptoms in girls and should provide treatment just as aggressively as they do when boys have ADHD. Parents need to take ADHD symptoms in girls seriously as well and should seek help early.

Summary

ADHD is a neurobiological disorder that affects between five and seven percent of children and between one and three percent of adults. The diagnosis of ADHD has increased over the past twenty years due to greater awareness of this condition and its impact on the lives of sufferers. The core symptoms of ADHD are inattention, hyperactivity, and impulsivity. There are three types of ADHD: predominantly inattentive type, predominantly hyperactive-impulsive type, and combined type. Children with the inattentive type tend to have problems primarily with focus and concentration that can seriously impact academic performance. These children tend to be identified later than those who are the hyperactive-impulsive or the combined type. Children with the hyperactive-impulsive and combined type often have serious disruptive behavior disorders such as oppositional disorder or conduct disorder. Many children with ADHD, regardless of type, can have other co-occurring problems such as learning disorders, anxiety, depression, and low self-esteem. Girls with ADHD are under diagnosed, but they often have serious social and academic impairments similar to boys with ADHD.

Chapter 2   Associated Problems or Co-Morbid Disorders

As if ADHD weren't enough of a problem in and of itself, children with ADHD typically also have other behavioral, emotional, or learning disorders. The most common of these are oppositional defiant disorder, conduct disorder, depression, and anxiety. Other disorders which can co-occur with ADHD are learning disabilities, speech and language problems, fine-motor incoordination, motor tics, and Tourette's syndrome. Obviously, the presence of these co-occurring problems complicates the diagnosis and treatment.

Oppositional Defiant Disorder

For as long as the Nelsons could remember, Jack was always a strong-willed child. His grandfather used to call him the "mule" because there would be no way you could stop him once he made up his mind to do something. Any attempt to persuade him would be met with a temper outburst or argument which would wreak havoc within the family.

Up to forty percent of children and as many as sixty-five percent of adolescents with ADHD exhibit such degrees of stubbornness and noncompliance they fall into a category of disruptive behavior disorder known as oppositional defiant disorder. Children and teens with oppositional defiant disorder are described by their parents as difficult to manage. They may exhibit frequent temper outbursts. They can be strong-willed and argumentative with adults. They may actively defy or refuse adult requests or rules and they often blame others for their own mistakes. They are touchy or easily annoyed by others, angry and resentful, spiteful, and may swear or use obscene language.

To be diagnosed as having oppositional defiant disorder, the child must have a pattern of negative, hostile, and defiant behavior which lasts at least six months. The behavior pattern must cause significant impairment in social, academic, or occupational functioning. During this time, at least four of the behavioral characteristics listed below must be present.

Characteristics of oppositional defiant disorder:
1. often loses temper
2. often argues with adults
3. often actively defies or refuses to comply with adults' requests or rules
4. often deliberately annoys people
5. often blames others for his or her mistakes or misbehavior
6. is often touchy or easily annoyed by others
7. is often angry and resentful
8. is often spiteful or vindictive

Children with oppositional defiant disorder can have a devastating effect on their family. Parents get fatigued under the constant pressure of trying to manage difficult behavior. Communication between parent and the child usually is quite negative and coercive. The parents yell a great deal and the child continuously defies them. This pattern of defiance may go on for several years.

As you can imagine, when ADHD and oppositional defiant disorder co-occur, the problems can multiply. If the child with ADHD is treated early there is a good chance symptoms of defiance will improve. Parents can learn behavior management strategies to manage the behavior better. An excellent book for parents to learn management of oppositional children was written by Russell Barkley. *The Defiant Child* helps parents understand the causes of oppositional and defiant behavior and takes parents through a step-by-step program of managing difficult behavior. Many of these strategies come from traditional parent training programs and were adapted for children with ADHD by Barkley. These strategies are reviewed in chapter 6.

Medications to treat ADHD symptoms can also reduce defiance. Educational interventions to treat ADHD can relieve school pressures resulting in improvements in attitude and behavior.

Conduct Disorder
Conduct disorder co-occurs with ADHD in about thirty percent of children and adolescents referred for treatment. Adolescents with conduct disorder may exhibit behavior that is characterized by aggression toward people and animals, destruction of property, deceitfulness or theft, and serious violation of rules. To be diagnosed as having conduct disorder, the child must have a pattern of behavior in which the basic rights of others or major social norms or rules are violated. There must be the presence of at least three of the following characteristics within the past year with at least one characteristic present in the last six months.

Characteristics of conduct disorder:
Aggression to people and animals
1. often bullies, threatens, or intimidates others

2. often initiates physical fights
3. has used a weapon that can cause serious physical harm to others (e.g., a bat, brick, broken bottle, knife, gun)
4. has been physically cruel to people
5. has been physically cruel to animals
6. has stolen while confronting a victim (e.g., mugging, purse snatching, extortion, armed robbery
7. has forced someone into sexual activity

Destruction of property
8. has deliberately engaged in fire setting with the intention of causing serious damage
9. has deliberately destroyed others' property (other than by fire setting)

Deceitfulness or theft
10. has broken into someone else's house, building, or car
11. often lies to obtain goods or favors or to avoid obligations
12. has stolen items of nontrivial value without confronting a victim (e.g., shoplifting, but without breaking and entering; forgery)

Serious violations of rules
13. often stays out at night despite parental prohibition, beginning before age thirteen years
14. has run away from home overnight at least twice while living in parental or parental surrogate home (or once without returning for a lengthy period)
15. often truant from school, beginning before age thirteen years

The severity of conduct disorder ranges from mild to severe based on the number of symptoms demonstrated and the degree of harm rendered to person or property. There are two broad groups of children with conduct disorder. In one group are children who had an early onset of symptoms of conduct disorder. Those in this group developed symptoms before age ten. They are more likely to have antisocial behavior problems throughout life. In the second group are children who had a later onset of symptoms of conduct disorder. Those in this group developed symptoms after the age of ten. Their antisocial problems are not as chronic and persistent and are not likely to continue beyond adolescence.

As with oppositional defiant disorder, when ADHD and conduct disorder co-occur, problems can multiply. Early intervention is extremely important to prevent serious antisocial behavior, substance abuse, and potential delinquency. Parents will benefit from learning behavior management strategies. Treatment with medication can improve symptoms of aggression, defiance, and irritability as well as targeting ADHD symptoms. Educational interventions can reduce stress on the child and may make school a more positive experience.

Depression
Children with ADHD may be at greater risk for developing depressive disorders than non-ADHD children. One type of depression children or adolescents may develop is known as

dysthymia. Children and teens with dysthymia have low mood most of the day, more often than not, for at least one year. Their low mood may take the form of irritability. In addition, they may have symptoms of poor appetite or overeating, insomnia or hypersomnia, low energy, low self-esteem, poor concentration, and feelings of hopelessness.

Another type of depression children and adolescents may develop is known as major depression. Those with major depression have depressed mood most of the day and nearly every day for at least two weeks. Other symptoms include: deriving little or no pleasure from activities; significant weight loss when not dieting or less weight gain than expected; insomnia or hypersomnia nearly every day; low energy; feelings of worthlessness or inappropriate guilt nearly every day; diminished ability to think, concentrate, or make decisions; and recurrent thoughts of death.

Dr. Joseph Biederman and his colleagues found that having ADHD increases the risk for developing manic-depressive illness, also known as bipolar disorder. Eleven percent of the children with ADHD they studied had bipolar disorder at the start of their study and an additional twelve percent developed bipolar disorder four years later. Children with bipolar disorder have frequent and rapid dramatic shifts of mood including elation, depression, irritability, and anger. At times they may have an exaggerated positive view of themselves, believing they are right and others are wrong. Their speech may become "pressured," marked by intense rapid talking and accompanied by "racing thoughts" they cannot control. In addition to the symptoms noted above, a family history of bipolar disorder, severe symptoms of ADHD, oppositional disorder, and conduct disorder are markers that could signal the presence of bipolar disorder.

Anxiety Disorders

Children and adolescents with ADHD are more likely to have anxiety related disorders than those not affected by ADHD. Two types of anxiety disorders that occur in children are separation anxiety disorder and overanxious disorder. To be diagnosed as having separation anxiety disorder, the child must have the following characteristics for more than four weeks.

Characteristics of separation anxiety disorder:
1. recurrent, excessive distress when separated from home or a major attachment figure occurs or is anticipated
2. persistent and excessive worry about losing, or about possible harm befalling, major attachment figures
3. persistent and excessive worry that an untoward event will lead to separation from a major attachment figure (e.g., getting lost or being kidnapped)
4. persistent reluctance or refusal to go to school or elsewhere because of fear of separation
5. persistently and excessively fearful or reluctant to be alone without major attachment figures at home or without significant adults in other settings
6. persistent reluctance or refusal to go to sleep without being near a major attachment figure or to sleep away from home

7. repeated nightmares involving the theme of separation
8. repeated complaints of physical symptoms (such as headaches, stomachaches, nausea, or vomiting) when separation from major attachment figures occurs or is anticipated

Overanxious disorder of childhood may exist if there is excessive anxiety and worry about a number of events or activities (such as school) occurring more days than not for at least six months. The child with this type of anxiety disorder finds it difficult to control worrying and may have some of the following additional symptoms: restlessness or feeling keyed up or on edge; becoming easily fatigued; difficulty concentrating or their mind going blank; irritability; muscle tension; and a sleep disturbance that can cause difficulty falling asleep, staying asleep, or having a restful sleep.

Treatment for children with ADHD who also have an anxiety disorder must address both conditions. These children need support, reassurance, and encouragement. Antidepressant and anxiolytic medications may improve their mood, reduce anxiety, and also help with some ADHD symptoms. Stimulant medications may increase anxiety in some children.

Learning Problems

Up to twenty-five percent of children with ADHD show evidence of a learning disability. A learning disability is a deficit in one or more of the basic psychological processes involved in understanding or using spoken or written language. These problems are often the result of language impairments, perceptual dysfunctions, or disturbances in the way information is processed and expressed in written or oral communications. Learning disabled students may show weaknesses in reading, writing, spelling, or arithmetic skills. In addition, children with ADHD may have trouble planning, organizing, and completing work. They may not be able to sustain attention to assignments. They may require more time to complete work. They may not read instructions carefully or may make careless errors.

Obsessive-Compulsive Disorder

Some children with obsessive-compulsive disorder also have ADHD.

Characteristics of obsessive-compulsive disorder:
1. intrusive, forceful, and repetitive thoughts, images, or sounds that are lodged in one's mind and cannot be willfully eliminated
2. compulsions to perform motor or mental acts
3. excessive and recurrent doubting about matters of either major or minor importance

The obsessions or compulsions cause marked distress, are time consuming, and significantly interfere with normal functioning. Examples of obsessive or compulsive behavior in children may include: overconcern with cleanliness, repeated hand washing, unusual or overly rigid eating habits, excessive concern about the tidiness of their room and their belongings, compulsion to place items around the house in a particular way, repeated checking if something is on or off, locked or unlocked, ritualistic counting, or repetition of a series of acts before moving on to something else.

Treatment for obsessive-compulsive disorder usually involves a combination of medication and behavior therapy. When ADHD is also present, the treatment can become much more complicated. Multiple medications may be prescribed to treat both disorders.

Asperger's Disorder

Asperger's disorder is an impairment in social interaction, that was first described in the 1940s. Children with Asperger's have impaired social interactions and unusual patterns of communication and behavior.

When communicating, they exhibit some of the following symptoms: a marked impairment in nonverbal behaviors used to communicate with others such as eye contact, facial expression, body postures, and gestures; failure to develop friendships appropriate to one's age and development; failure to seek out others to communicate; and lack of social reciprocity when interacting with others. In contrast, the ADHD child's social behavior is affected by impulsivity and failure to read social cues because they are not concentrating on the reactions of others.

Those with Asperger's also exhibit unusual behavior patterns including preoccupation with a specific interest, inflexible adherence to specific routines or rituals, repetitive motor mannerisms (such as hand or finger flapping or twisting or whole body movements), and preoccupation with parts of objects.

Asperger's disorder is not as common as ADHD and is not frequently seen in those with ADHD. However, some people with Asperger's also have problems with hyperactivity, impulsivity, and inattention. For some, this may be caused by the Asperger's itself, while others may have a co-diagnosis of ADHD.

Speech and Language Problems

Children with ADHD tend to have a greater amount of speech and language problems than those not affected by ADHD. Young ADHD children are more likely to have delays in normal speech development problems with articulation of sounds, and sequencing thoughts. As they become older, problems with organizing and planning what to say are more frequent. Problems with language can also lead to difficulties with written expression, reading fluency, and comprehension.

Sensory and Motor Problems

Hearing and vision problems are not more prevalent in children with ADHD than they are within the general childhood population. However, as many as fifty percent of ADHD children are reported to have problems with motor coordination, especially on tasks requiring fine-motor coordination. They are often noted to have problems with handwriting. They often write more slowly than other children and they tend to dislike and avoid assignments where there is a lot of writing required.

Social Adjustment Problems

It is estimated that more than fifty percent of children with ADHD have some type of social relationship problems. Observers report hyperactive children to be much more aggressive, disruptive, bossy, noisy, intrusive, and socially inappropriate. They experience higher rates of social rejection from peers. They are more likely to view events that happen to them as not being their fault, and they may blame others too quickly. These traits probably follow them through their teen years.

Those with ADHD-inattentive type may have different social problems. These children are by nature more passive, quiet, and non-competitive than their peers. While they are better accepted by peers than those children with ADHD who are hyperactive and impulsive, they often remain on the outskirts of social relationships. They can be quiet and shy, which keeps them from initiating interaction with others.

Transient Tics

Transient tics are sudden, repetitive, and involuntary movements of muscles. Vocal tics involve muscles that control speech and cause involuntary sounds such as coughing, throat clearing, sniffing, making loud sounds, grunting, or calling out words. Motor tics involve other muscles and can occur in any part of the body. Some examples of motor tics are eye blinking, shoulder shrugging, facial grimacing, head jerking, and a variety of hand movements. Tics that are less common involve self-injurious behavior such as hitting or biting oneself and coprolalia (involuntary use of profane words or gestures). When these types of tics occur many times a day, nearly every day for at least four weeks, but for no longer than twelve consecutive months, the child may have a transient tic disorder.

It is estimated that ten percent of children and adolescents with ADHD will develop a transient tic disorder. Others may develop a tic disorder that is associated with the use of stimulant medication.

Chronic Tics and Tourette's Syndrome

A child who has either a motor or a vocal tic (but not both), which occurs many times a day, nearly every day, for a period of at least one year (without stopping for more than three months), may be diagnosed as having a chronic tic disorder. Tourette's syndrome is a chronic tic disorder characterized by both multiple motor tics and one or more vocal tics, although not necessarily concurrent. These tics are more severe than the simple, transient motor tics described earlier. They occur many times a day, nearly every day, or intermittently throughout a period of more than one year. They involve the head and frequently other parts of the body such as the torso, arms, and legs. Vocal tics may include the production of sounds like clucking, grunting, yelping, barking, snorting, and coughing. Utterances of obscenities, coprolalia, are rare and occur in about ten percent of children with Tourette's.

Cigarette Smoking and Substance Use Disorder

Adolescents who smoke cigarettes have a five times greater likelihood of using drugs than non-smokers. Studies by Dr. Joseph Biederman and his colleagues at Massachusetts General Hospital, found ADHD subjects were more likely to be smokers (nineteen percent in the ADHD group vs ten percent in a normal control group), and they started smoking at an earlier age. These investigators also found cigarette smoking increases in adolescents with ADHD as the number of co-morbid disorders they have increases. The rate of cigarette smoking was ten percent in ADHD adolescents with no co-morbid disorders, twenty-one percent in those with one co-morbid disorder, thirty-five percent in those with two co-morbid disorders, and forty percent when ADHD and three other disorders (depression, anxiety, and conduct disorder) were present.

Several studies looking at the co-morbidity of substance use disorder and ADHD in adolescence indicated that the presence of ADHD alone does not increase the risk of developing a substance use disorder. However, ADHD plus conduct disorder does.

Sleep Problems

Excessive movement during sleep, once thought to be a characteristic of those with ADHD, is no longer one of the criteria used in considering a diagnosis. However, research conducted on the sleep behavior of children with ADHD consistently notes that parents report greater sleep problems in ADHD children than in non-ADHD children. These reports indicate that more than fifty percent of ADHD children need more time to fall asleep, nearly forty percent may have problems with frequent night wakings, and more than fifty percent have trouble waking in the morning.

Summary

Children with ADHD frequently have co-occurring problems. Disorders involving disruptive behavior, such as oppositional defiant disorder, are the most common co-occurring conditions found in children with the combined and hyperactive-impulsive type of ADHD. In addition, a significant number of children with ADHD also suffer from mood disorders such as depression and problems with anxiety. Learning problems associated with speech and language disorders, problems with reading, mathematics, and writing, as well as school performance problems, are common. Difficulties with fine-motor incoordination, simple motor tics, chronic tics, and Tourette's syndrome are also associated with ADHD. While children with ADHD are at no greater risk for developing disorders such as obsessive-compulsive disorder or Asperger's disorder, a significant number of children with these conditions do have ADHD.

It is the exception rather than the rule if a child with ADHD doesn't have any co-occurring problems. Professionals assessing children for ADHD should look for the presence of conditions discussed above. As a parent, you should ensure that treatments provided to your child, target all aspects of their problems. Children with ADHD who have co-existing learning problems, for example, should recieve help for their learning difficulties as well as for their ADHD symptoms. Often, the ADHD symptoms are the most easily treated.

Chapter 3   Across the Lifespan

More often than not, symptoms of ADHD will continue through the childhood, adolescence and into the adult lives of many people diagnosed as youngsters. Obviously, the manifestation of symptoms differs across the lifespan. ADHD affects young children far differently than it does adults and the impact of symptoms, resulting impairment, and methods of treatment vary by age and level of development. This section looks at ADHD at different stages of development: preschool, middle childhood, adolescence, and adulthood.

Early Childhood

It is customary for preschool age children to be overactive and impulsive from time to time. Their attention is captured by things that interest them, but usually for short periods of time. They shift quickly from one activity to another. We expect preschoolers to be somewhat demanding, impulsive, or self-centered and generally we don't get too upset when they get frustrated and have occasional temper outbursts or crying spells. Hopefully, we anticipate their frustration, plan for their short attention span, and vary their activities enough to sustain their interest.

At what point does activity exceed the bounds of normalcy and become hyperactivity? When is inattentiveness considered attention deficit? At what age should we expect immaturity to end and impulsivity to disappear? Unfortunately there are no objective answers to these questions. Healthcare professionals must be careful to differentiate normal preschooler social behavior from the hyperactive, impulsive, and "over the top" behavior characteristic of preschoolers with ADHD.

It is estimated athat about two percent of children ages three to five have ADHD. In 2001, George DuPaul and his colleagues at Lehigh University studied preschool-age children with ADHD. They found that those with ADHD were rated as less socially skilled than non-ADHD preschoolers. At home, they were twice as likely to be noncompliant to commands and their parents were three times more likely to exhibit negative behavior towards them. In the classroom, the ADHD preschoolers were much more likely to have negative social interactions, especially during unstructured, free-play activities. They also had weaker academic skills as compared to a non-ADHD comparison group.

Unfortunately, in many preschoolers these symptoms do not seem to improve with age and maturation. Dr. Susan Campbell studied three-year-olds with a pattern of hyperactive, impulsive, and related disruptive behavior. Nearly one half continued to experience behavioral problems by school age, and nearly one-third received a diagnosis of ADHD. Dr. John Lavigne and others at the Children's Memorial Hospital in Chicago found that in more than fifty percent of cases, preschool children's disruptive behavior persisted up to four years from the time they were first identified as having a behavior problem. Another study found that boys described as hard to manage at age three or four had about a sixty-seven percent chance of continuing problems two years later.

Parents of ADHD preschoolers often describe themselves as exhausted by the child-rearing process. For very hyperactive preschoolers typical methods of discipline such as time-out, positive reinforcement, and punishment don't work well. They may try to discipline their youngsters and teach appropriate behavior, but the child seems unable to maintain self-control. Parents are often left without an effective means to manage behavior. Teachers of ADHD preschoolers end up equally frustrated. Disruptive behavior, especially aggression toward other children, becomes a chief concern for the teacher. Parents of the more seriously involved kids are frequently asked to withdraw their child from the preschool only to end up in a desperate search for another school that will be able to handle their child's problems. Frequently the parent ends up relying on the good graces of another preschool director or teacher who is willing to give their child a second (or third) chance.

Stimulants are routinely used to treat ADHD in school-age children and increasingly in preschool children. Preschoolers with ADHD are being treated with stimulants for extended periods of time although there has been very little research on the effects of stimulants in young children. Findings from the limited research indicate that about seventy-five percent of ADHD preschoolers respond to stimulants, showing improvement in core ADHD symptoms. However, the preschool child on stimulants will need close monitoring because of frequent side effects that require dosage adjustment. Also, due to the high rate of associated health problems in the preschool child with ADHD, clinicians and parents will need to watch for drug interactions or additive side effects with concurrently prescribed medications.

Middle Childhood

Many children with ADHD will be identified by the time they are nine or ten years of age. If the child is primarily inattentive, but not necessarily hyperactive, he will leave a trail of unfinished tasks: uncovered toothpaste in the bathroom, clothes scattered about the floor of the bedroom, bed unmade, toys and books left wherever they were last used, games started and unfinished, tomorrow's math homework paper mixed in with last month's spelling, dresser drawers bulging from unfolded clothes, and on and on.

If hyperactivity and impulsivity are also present, the picture at home becomes even more chaotic: toys scattered and broken, walls marked up, frequent family arguments over listening, meals disrupted by fighting, shopping trips marred by relentless demands, sibling conflicts, and frayed nerves.

Patterns of academic frustration and failure, social rejection and criticism from parents and teachers can build in elementary school and symptoms of other disorders associated with ADHD may begin to appear. Approximately sixty percent of these children will develop oppositional defiant disorder. Frustrated by their lack of success, these children may become irritable and sullen. About half of this group of oppositional children will develop an even more serious behavior disorder in adolescence, namely conduct disorder. Many ADHD children will suffer low self-esteem due to their inability to achieve the same levels of success as their peers. Still others will develop depression.

It is at this time that children are most likely to be referred for an assessment after which a diagnosis is given and treatment is started. Children with the hyperactive-impulsive or combined types of ADHD are much more likely to be referred by their teachers and parents for an evaluation. Because their disruptive behavior adds stress to their family and their classroom, parents and teachers become alarmed. The child with the inattentive type of ADHD may go unnoticed, but nevertheless may struggle with school work, may have trouble staying focused and organized, and may not be able to keep up academically or socially.

After making a diagnosis, the physician may try different medications to see which are most effective. Strength of dosing and time of dosing will be modified based on the child's individual response to the medications. The child's parents become educated about ADHD for the first time and learn about the benefits and risks of taking medication. Parents frequently take on a more formal role as their child's advocate in school. Mothers and fathers help the teacher plan accommodations in the classroom, seek information from the teacher about their child's progress, and work closely with their child to ensure that the child is completing assigned work in an organized and responsible way.

Also at this time, co-morbid problems appear as the child may struggle in school and in social surroundings. The child and the parent may visit a psychologist, social worker, or counselor to manage behavior and emotions. Parents may provide more structure at home by implementing behavioral treatments. The child may be taught self-control strategies. Close communication between parents, healthcare professionals and teachers is essential to make certain that treatments are addressing the child's needs appropriately and effectively.

Adolescence

As many as eighty percent of children diagnosed with ADHD in middle childhood will continue to have symptoms of overactivity, inattention, and impulsivity through adolescence. Longitudinal studies following groups of children with ADHD into their adolescent years consistently find that teens with ADHD have higher rates of disruptive and non-disruptive problems including anxiety, depression, oppositional behavior, and school failure. The rate of substance abuse is also higher, but this is usually found in those teens who have more severe conduct problems.

School problems can intensify in middle and high school. Greater demands are placed on students in secondary schools. They have more teachers to cope with, more work to be responsible for, more activities to organize and they tend to be less closely supervised by teachers and parents. The ADHD adolescent starts middle school with several teachers each of whom probably has two hundred or more students to teach. It is easy to get lost in the shuffle.

Raising an adolescent with ADHD is challenging to parents and other family members. There is likely to be more conflict between the ADHD teenager and parent. This is much more prevalent, however, when the adolescent with ADHD has additional problems related to substance abuse, delinquency or learning difficulties or when there is other stress or adversity in the family.

Adolescents with ADHD present a significant challenge for the doctors and counselors that treat them. As the demands of school, social life, and responsibilities in general increase in adolescence and the number of co-morbid diagnoses increase, healthcare professionals are faced with a mountain of problems that may be difficult for the teen, the doctor or the parent to manage. ADHD teens are at risk for more driving crashes when they get their licenses. Teenagers with ADHD are often unwilling to accept responsibility for their behavior. They may be reluctant to accept medical treatments. They may refuse to take the ADHD medication they willingly took during childhood and may be adverse to accepting other treatments as well (e.g., seeing a counselor, getting extra academic help, working with a tutor).

Adulthood

Within the past twenty years, the persistence of ADHD into adulthood has been increasingly recognized. Unfortunately, compared to studies of children, there are relatively few studies of adults with ADHD. Many of these studies have focused on issues related to the identification of the disorder, the presence of other psychiatric disorders in adults with ADHD, and the use of medication treatments. There seem to be more questions than answers.

- The prevalence of adults with ADHD is still uncertain. Figures vary depending on what criteria is used and who is reporting symptoms.

- There is a lack of consensus on the specific diagnostic criteria that should be used for adults with ADHD. The procedures that have been developed for evaluating ADHD in adults include self-reports of both current and past symptoms as well as collaborative reports of the same symptoms from parents and/or spouses. Checklists, interviews, and review of past records (i.e., school report cards, transcripts, medical records). The wording of the ADHD criteria in the DSM-IV is appropriate for children but not for adults. Existing protocols have been modified by changing the wording of symptoms and the number of symptoms required for cutoffs (Murphy & Barkley, 1996).

- The presence of other co-morbid disorders such as anxiety, depression, bipolar disorder, etc. can cause additional confusion to a greater degree than when making a diagnosis in childhood. Differentiating ADHD from these other mental disorders in adults can be difficult. Many of the symptoms of adult ADHD are also found in other disorders. For example, difficulty concentrating is also characteristic of people with anxiety disorders and mood disorders.

Dr. Sam Goldstein explains that the picture of ADHD in adulthood can be very variable. He divides adults with histories of ADHD into three categories: (1) those who seem to function fairly normally as adults although they have had childhood ADHD; (2) those who continue to have significant problems with ADHD as well as life difficulty involving work, interpersonal relations, self-esteem, anxiety and emotional lability; and (3) those who develop serious psychiatric and anti-social problems and are quite dysfunctional. The sections that follow contain outcome information about academic and occupational functioning, social skills, and family functioning in adults with ADHD.

Academic and occupational attainment. Adults with childhood histories of ADHD and/or a diagnosis of ADHD made in adulthood, on average, have more difficulty achieving in school and in their employment. They are less likely to go on to higher education and are more likely to be employed in skilled labor positions and to change jobs more often. Adults with ADHD may do better in occupations that are fast-paced and involve risk-taking and an outgoing style of communication. These job characteristics seem to match the characteristics found in many adults with ADHD.

<u>Social skills</u>. A few studies have looked at how adults with ADHD function in social interactions. Symptoms such as inattention and impulsivity are likely to contribute to social difficulties. Adults with ADHD are often described as having difficulty with the give and take of conversation. They may ramble on, unaware of cues given off by the person they are talking with that they should alter the style of their communication. Drs. Gabrielle Weiss and Lilly Hechtman (1993) found that young adults in the ADHD group they studied were significantly worse at social skills in job interviews and other situations that required assertiveness and oral communication. Dr. Michele Novotni, in her book, *What Does Everybody Else Know That I Don't?*, gives many illustrations of how ADHD symptoms can impact adult social interaction and offers strategies for improvement.

<u>Family functioning</u>. Due to the high heritability of ADHD, adults with ADHD who become parents are more likely to have children who also have ADHD. As a result, these parents have a double challenge. They must manage their own ADHD symptoms and they must help their child manage theirs. ADHD can interfere with a parent's patience and ability to use effective parenting strategies. Children with ADHD have a greater need for a parent who has a clear and consistent parenting style and established routines and structure in the home. Parents may have to implement different behavioral treatment programs requiring consistent delivery of rewards and consequences. They may have to be good time managers to keep their ADHD child on track so they have time for schoolwork, household responsibilities, and recreation. Often treatment of ADHD symptoms in a parent leads to improvements in parenting skills. Unfortunately, ADHD may have a negative impact on marital stability as higher rates of separation and divorce have been found in adults with ADHD. *Moms with ADD: A Self-Help Manual* by Christine Adamec and *Voices from Fatherhood: Fathers, Sons and ADHD* by Patrick Kilcarr and Patricia Quinn, offer many tips for parents, particularly if they suffer from ADHD as well.

Summary

ADHD can be a lifetime disorder. About half of children diagnosed will continue to have symptoms of ADHD in adulthood. Of course the manifestation of symptoms changes with age. Preschoolers which ADHD, combined type and hyperactive-impulsive type are usually diagnosed early because of their disruptive behavior. If they are very hyperactive and impulsive they may also exhibit aggressive behavior which causes serious problems in a preschool setting. In middle childhood, more children with the inattentive type are seen as a result of greater demands placed on the child for attention and work completion. In adolescence, hyperactivity begins to settle down in exchange for restlessness and fidgety behavior. Other problems with self-esteem, mood, and conduct may become paramount. Girls with ADHD, in particular may develop emotional difficulties associated with low mood, irritability, poor self-esteem, and anxiety or depression. ADHD can become a serious problem in adulthood as well. Job performance, academic attainment, and social functioning can become affected. We are more aware than ever of the fact that ADHD can be a serious lifelong problem and treatments that were once thought to be exclusively in the domain of childhood and adolescence are now being effectively used to help adults with ADHD.

Chapter 4 Causes of ADHD

More than a hundred years ago, Dr. George Still, an English pediatrician, gave us the first clues as to the causes of ADHD. At a meeting of the Royal College of Physicians, Still noted that symptoms of restlessness, inattention, and overarousal in certain children were likely the result of brain damage and other factors such as heredity and environment. In the early 1900s it was presumed that these brain injuries stemmed from infections such as encephalitis and meningitis. This was supported following a 1917-1918 worldwide epidemic of influenza with encephalitis wherein some recovering children had symptoms of restlessness, inattention, and impulsivity. Other children with similar symptoms, who had no history of infection, were presumed to have suffered some form of head injury or complication of pregnancy or delivery.

Virtually all articles in scientific journals and textbooks assume that ADHD behaviors of hyperactivity, inattention, and impulsivity are largely or entirely due to abnormal brain functioning. ADHD is frequently referred to as a neurobehavioral disorder, neurobiological disorder, or a neurological disorder. In a moment, we will take a look at some of the studies that point to ADHD as a brain-based disorder, however, it would be wise to keep in mind that there are other (non-neurological) factors that can affect the expression of ADHD behavior. These can include environmental and social influences.

Certain areas of the brain control our ability to pay attention, plan, organize, inhibit impulses, organize, and remember. These functions are vital to effective self-management and problem-solving. They are often referred to as "executive functions." The frontal regions of the brain are presumed to control executive functioning. The frontal regions are highly interconnected with the limbic (motivational) system, the reticular activating (arousal) system, the posterior association cortex (perceptual/cognitive processes and knowledge base), and the motor (action) regions. From infancy on, we see maturation of executive functioning in the form of attention control, problem-solving ability, self-regulation of emotion and behavior, and the development of goal-directed behavior and self-monitoring. Eighteen-month-old children show the ability to control their actions and inhibit behavior to obtain a goal well beyond what they were able to do as infants. With every passing year the brain matures and our executive function processes grow stronger, reaching maximum development in adulthood. The development of executive functions may be affected by abnormalities in neurotransmission, structure, and function in certain areas of the brain. In people with ADHD, development of executive functions lags behind and often never fully develops to the extent found in those who do not have ADHD.

Brain Injury

Head injuries sustained as a result of automobile accidents, falls, or other head trauma can result in impairments in cognitive and behavioral functioning. When such injuries affect the frontal regions of the brain the result can be disturbances in attention, hyperactivity, and self-control. Animal studies have also helped us identify the frontal region of the brain as being involved in ADHD-like symptoms. Chimpanzees, for example, were trained to perform certain psychological tests then scientists disabled the frontal region of their brains through surgery or other means and repeated the tests and observed their behavior. When the frontal region of the brain was altered, the chimpanzees showed behavior patterns that were quite similar to children with ADHD. They became more hyperactive, impulsive, and less able to pay attention for long periods of time. They could not inhibit their behavior and had social problems with other animals. When other areas of the brain were altered, these patterns of ADHD-like behavior did not appear. However, less than ten percent of children with ADHD can be shown to have suffered brain injuries. This has led scientists to conjecture that something else may be affecting the development of this part of the brain.

Brain Chemistry

Many scientists have implicated neurotransmitters (chemicals in the brain that enable nerve cells to transmit information to other nerve cells) as a cause of ADHD. The brain is a complex information network made up of billions of nerve cells called neurons which transmit information to each other in much the same way as signals are transmitted electronically in a telecommunications network. However, messages within the brain are transferred by electrical conduction within a nerve cell and by chemical conduction between nerve cells. Once a message is carried along the axon (cell body) of a sending nerve cell, it has to cross a small space called a synapse to reach a receiving cell. At the tip of the axon are tiny sacs that contain neurotransmitter chemicals which are automatically released by the sending nerve cell. These neurotransmitter chemicals excite the receiving nerve cell, causing that cell to fire and thus once again propel the message along the axon to receptors in the next nerve cell. Once the message is received the neurotransmitter chemical is deactivated or taken up from the synapse and stored in sacs so as not to cause repeated firing of the receiving cell.

Dopamine, norepinephrine, and serotonin are examples of neurotransmitter chemicals that play an important part in brain activity. They make up the dopaminergic, noradrenergic, and serotonergic chemical systems. These systems regulate our senses, thinking, perception, mood, attention, and behavior. The malfunction of any of these neurotransmitter systems can have a wide ranging impact on how a child behaves and learns.

Support for the idea that brain chemistry is responsible for ADHD comes from a number of sources:

- Certain drugs (stimulants and nonstimulants such as atomoxetine), known to affect neurotransmitters such as those listed above, can temporarily improve the ability of children with ADHD to regulate behavior and attention.
- These drugs increase the amount of these neurotransmitters in the brain.
- At least two genes that regulate dopamine have been identified as being associated with ADHD. One of these genes is involved in removing dopamine from the synapse between neurons and the other affects the sensitivity of neurons to the dopamine itself.

Brain Activity

Studies using electroencephalography (EEG) while children with ADHD were sitting at rest and also while they were performing certain mental tasks, have found that there was lower brain activity in the frontal region. Other studies found there was less blood flow in the frontal region, particularly in the caudate nucleus, an important structure in the pathway between the most frontal portion of the brain and the structures in the middle of the brain known as the limbic system. These areas are important in inhibiting behavior and sustaining attention. Dr. Alan Zametkin, using positron emission tomography (PET) found that adults with ADHD had less brain activity, particularly in the frontal lobe. This study was repeated with twenty adolescents with ADHD and Zametkin again found reduced activity in the frontal region, more on the left side than the right. Other studies have found that when children were given drugs that lower brain activity, such as phenobarbital and dilantin, problems with inattention and hyperactivity increase.

Brain Structure

In the past ten to fifteen years, magnetic resonance imaging (MRI) studies have found differences in the brain structure of people with ADHD. Drs. George Hynd and his colleagues at the University of Georgia (1991) found that the caudate nucleus of children with ADHD was somewhat larger on the right side than on the left. Dr. Hynd and his colleagues also found, in other studies, that the corpus callosum, a large band of nerve fibers that connects the right and left sides of the brain, was somewhat smaller in children with ADHD than in children without

ADHD. Additional studies by Xavier Castellanos and Jay Giedd (1997) and Pauline Filipek (1997), and their colleagues found further evidence of smaller brain regions (structures in the basal ganglia and certain regions on the right side of the cerebellum) in children with ADHD.

The Role of Genetics

Family, twin, adoption, and molecular genetic studies offer strong evidence of the important role that genetics play in the risk for ADHD. Relatives of individuals with ADHD have a greater risk for ADHD. Drs. Stephen Faraone and Joseph Biederman have studied the familiality of ADHD and have found that siblings of children with ADHD have a two to three fold greater risk of ADHD than siblings of normal controls.

Twin studies are often used to sort out the degree of genetic influence on a trait or disorder. Twins can be monozygotic (MZ), identical twins who have all of their genes in common; or dizygotic (DZ), non-identical or fraternal twins who, on average, share half of their genes. If we accept that MZ and DZ twins share their environment to the same extent, then any greater similarity in MZ than DZ twins should reflect genetic effects. Twin studies done by Dr. Florence Levy in Australia found a much higher concordance of ADHD for monozygotic than dizygotic twins that is consistent with high heritability of ADHD.

Adoption studies provide another way to disentangle genes and the environment. In such studies, the adopted-away offspring of affected parents are studied and compared with control adoptees. Biological parents of ADHD individuals are more likely to exhibit ADHD or related disorders than are adoptive parents.

Molecular genetics research is still at an early stage in psychiatric disorders, but this is also true for much of the rest of internal medicine. It is proving difficult to identify susceptibility genes for multi-factorial disorders. However, the strong evidence of genetic effects, the effect of stimulant medication on children with ADHD, and the concentration of neurons rich in dopamine and norepinephrine in the neural areas involved in executive function led to investigation of the role of candidate genes involved in the noradrenergic and dopaminergic systems. Drs. Edwin Cook and Mark Stein as well as Dr. Gerald LaHoste and his team found that ADHD has been associated with the dopamine transporter gene (DAT1) and the dopamine D4 receptor gene. Presumably, mutations in the respective genes may give rise to ADHD.

Maternal Infection, Alcohol, or Substance Use During Pregnancy

In the past few decades, there has been a growing awareness of the ways in which substances ingested by the mother during pregnancy may have adverse effects on the fetus. The thalidomide tragedy, with its subsequent devastating effects in causing limb deformities, is the most dramatic example of this. Infection, alcohol, and recreational drug use during pregnancy have all been investigated.

The evidence on the role of maternal infections is greatest in the case of influenza as a contributory predisposing factor to schizophrenia. When influenza occurs during the second trimester, it is associated with an approximate doubling of the risk of schizophrenia. Maternal rubella has well-established devastating effects on fetal development, leading to mental retardation, blindness and deafness. Heavy consumption of alcohol in the first trimester is known to be associated with physical consequences to fetal development (fetal-alcohol syndrome) and has important psychological consequences, particularly in relation to patterns of inattention/over activity. Researchers have found an association between mothers who smoked tobacco products or used alcohol during their pregnancy and the development of behavior and learning problems in their children. Nicotine and alcohol can be toxic to developing brain tissue and may have sustained effects on the behavior of the children exposed to these substances at early ages. However, it is unlikely that such exposure accounts for differences in brain development in the vast majority of children with ADHD.

Traumatic Brain Injury

Injury to the head leading to traumatic brain injury (TBI) is a major cause of hospitalization, severe disability, and death in childhood. Approximately one in ten children will experience traumatic loss of consciousness during childhood. Annually, over 500,000 children are hospitalized following TBI, with 3,000 to 4,000 deaths resulting. An additional 15,000 of these children will require prolonged hospitalization, often with a poor outcome. The majority of head injuries, however, are of a mild nature with outpatient management or a simple overnight stay in the hospital being all the treatment needed.

Open-head injuries typically involve localized brain damage. Closed-head injuries, often the result of traffic accidents or falls, are more common, and typically involve widespread damage. Child abuse, unfortunately, is another fairly common cause of head injury. Psychiatric disorders develop in about half of the survivors of head injuries. Severe closed-head injury can result in a distinctive syndrome of social disinhibition. These disinhibited children are outspoken, forgetful, over-talkative, impulsive, or careless about their own cleanliness and appearance.

Keith O. Yeates (2005) and his colleagues conducted a study of the long-term affects on attention in children with TBI. The investigators relied on data collected as part of a prospective longitudinal study of children injured between the ages of six and twelve, including children with moderate to severe TBI and a comparison group of children with orthopedic injuries (OI) not involving the head. Parents completed standardized ratings of attention problems soon after the child's injury and again during a long-term follow-up assessment that occurred on average four years post-injury. The children were also administered neuropsychological tests at the long-term follow-up assessment that measured attention and executive functions.

As expected, children with severe TBI displayed deficits in both cognitive and behavioral aspects of attention compared with those with OI not involving the head. In addition, they were substantially more likely than children in the OI group to display clinically significant attention problems. Approximately twenty percent of the severe TBI group displayed symptoms consistent with a diagnosis of combined type ADHD where as only four percent of the OI group did so. These findings confirm previous research showing both cognitive deficits in attention and executive functions and increased behavioral symptoms of attention problems and ADHD after childhood TBI.

Environmental Contaminants

The most studied neurotoxicant is lead. It has been clearly established that exposure of fetuses and children to amounts of lead produces deficits in cognitive functioning. Dr. Herbert Needleman, a child and adolescent psychiatrist, is an expert in this area, and he and other researchers have discovered that lead exposure can cause problems with attention, language function, and social adjustment. Doctors have known of lead's toxic effects since the turn of the century. In 1904, the first article about childhood lead poisoning from paint appeared in an Australian medical journal. France and Austria banned the interior use of lead paint in 1909, but a United State's ban on residential use didn't come until 1978. At that time, studies showed that eighty-eight percent of U.S. children had elevated lead levels.

Dr. Needleman (1998) suggests that the elimination of lead poisoning would reduce cognitive and attention deficits in children. The greatest impact would occur among the economically and socially disadvantaged populations of children. Between 1976 and 1994, the mean blood lead concentration in children in the United States was reduced by almost eighty percent, in direct proportion to the amount of lead produced. While it does not seem likely that lead poisoning accounts for more than a very small portion of children with ADHD, an association between elevated blood lead levels and hyperactivity has been demonstrated in a number of studies.

Food Allergies

There are a number of controversial areas in medicine. ADHD, and it's relation to food allergy, is certainly one of them. One of the main proponents of the food allergy/ADHD connection is Dr. Doris Rapp, a pediatric allergist. Dr. Rapp observed that many children in her practice had significant physical and behavioral changes when exposed to certain foods. They may have red ear lobes, dark circles under their eyes, or glazed eyes after eating certain foods. These children could have tremendous swings in behavior and display hyperactivity.

Prior to Dr. Rapp, another allergist, Dr. Benjamin Feingold, was quite outspoken in his belief that food allergies play an important role in causing children to be hyperactive. Feingold's 1975 publication, *Why Your Child is Hyperactive*, advised parents to put their hyperactive children on an elimination diet wherein foods containing artificial flavorings, dyes, and natural salycilates would be avoided.

While there is some evidence for an effect of diet upon the behavior of certain predisposed individuals, researchers have found that the effect is rather small. In these studies, children with ADHD are given suspect foods one at a time and their behavior is observed and compared to placebo conditions. Generally, the foods involved vary from child to child and include "natural" foods such as eggs, wheat flour, and citrus fruit as well as "artificial" ones such as food dyes. The action appears to be on irritable and non-compliant behavior rather than specifically on ADHD. One can conclude only that parents who have noticed that diet affects their children's behavior are, probably, sometimes right. Prescription of the diet is not yet justified, however, families who wish to explore the possibility further should be supported.

Other Medical Conditions

Other medical conditions can cause symptoms that look like ADHD, but which really are not. Hyperthyroidism, a disorder resulting in overproduction of a hormone produced by an overactive thyroid gland, can result in accelerated heart rate and hyperactive behavior. Treatment with medication to reduce the production of thyroid hormone will improve this condition. There are some types of seizure disorders which result in episodic periods of inattention characterized by prolonged staring, brief loss of conscious awareness, eye blinking, and sometimes, tremor. While such occurrences can happen several times a day, the seizure disorder should not be mistaken for ADHD. In such cases where a seizure disorder is suspected, the child should receive a thorough neurological examination.

There are other psychiatric disorders, such as anxiety disorders, depression, or bipolar disorders, which can occur in children or adolescents. These disorders may result in ADHD-like characteristics but should not be confused for ADHD.

Mental retardation, autistic disorder, and Gilles de la Tourette syndrome are additional neuropsychiatric disorders which could produce symptoms of inattention, distractibility, and impulsivity and could be confused with ADHD.

Medication Side Effects

Certain medications may cause ADHD-like behavior. Phenobarbital and dilantin, anti-convulsants used to treat children with seizure disorders, may give rise to inattention and hyperactivity. Children taking theophylline for asthma treatment may exhibit signs of ADHD-like behavior due to the medication's side effects. These effects are short-lived and disappear when the medication wears off.

Familial Factors

A range of psychosocial factors are associated with ADHD, including maternal stress during pregnancy and poor quality or disrupted early caregiving as may be seen in children in institutions or foster care.

Studies investigating parenting style and methods of discipline in families of hyperactive and normal children do not indicate that parents, by virtue of their parent-child interactions, cause their children to develop ADHD. However, most people would agree that children who live in families which lack structure, routine, discipline, and order may have a greater likelihood of developing disruptive behavior disorders which can result in symptoms of inattention, impulsivity, and hyperactivity. Children from homes with chaotic family interactions will often demonstrate poor organizational skills, difficulty with self-regulation, failure to accept responsibility for their actions, and so on. Behavior of this sort, resulting from difficulties in family functioning should not be confused with ADHD.

Summary

ADHD is universally considered a neurological disorder among experts. However, it can have multiple causes. Most children with ADHD have probably inherited the disorder. A small number of children with ADHD were probably victims of head injury, infection, or illness that affected brain functioning. Neurological research is ongoing and promises to yield more definitive answers in the future. Research into dietary causes of ADHD have failed to be convincing as to any definitive role that food allergies play for other than a small percentage of children with ADHD-like symptoms. Other medical conditions and psychosocial factors can contribute to problems of children with ADHD or can cause problems that look like ADHD, but which are manifestations of other disorders.

Chapter 5 Getting a Good Assessment

Not all children who exhibit signs of inattention, hyperactivity, or impulsivity have ADHD. Children challenged by difficult schoolwork or who are preoccupied by problems with family, friends, or elsewhere may have trouble keeping their mind focused. Nervousness can produce restless, fidgeting behavior. Unmotivated students often do not complete assignments or pay attention. Certain medical conditions can result in inattention. Many of these problems are commonly found in children and should not be confused with ADHD. It is important to get a comprehensive assessment to determine if other factors may be causing or contributing to ADHD-like symptoms.

Difficulty with school assignments can cause inattention. Joseph had trouble in school ever since he transferred from Norcross Elementary across town to his new school. He used to be the first one in his class to raise his hand and answer questions, but now he hardly ever participates. This class seems further ahead of his last one. The other students seem brighter. He said his new teacher talks too fast and he has trouble keeping up. All this change is causing him to feel overwhelmed and anxious and he can't seem to keep his mind on his work.

Being worried or depressed can cause inattention. Susan's parents were recently separated. Since then her life hasn't been the same. Her father moved out and found an apartment, her mother got a new job with better pay, but longer hours, and Susan's grandmother moved in with them to help out. Susan misses her father and worries about him being alone. She frequently hears her mother telling others that they have financial problems, and she knows her mother doesn't like working so hard. Susan wishes things were back the way they were before her parents split up, but deep down inside she knows that won't happen. With all of these problems on her mind, Susan is having difficulty concentrating in school.

Some medications can cause inattention and hyperactivity. Jeff has suffered from asthma since he was a preschooler. It got so bad sometimes that breathing became very difficult. Things got better after his doctor diagnosed his condition and gave him medication which improved his breathing. However, whenever he takes the asthma medication he gets "hyper" and gets in trouble in school.

Students who are learning English as a second language may have trouble paying attention. English is a second language for Ana. She just moved to this country from South America and her family always spoke Spanish. She's having a hard time catching on in seventh grade and most of the time she doesn't understand the teacher or the other students. Her mind wanders, and she often cannot force herself to pay attention to things she doesn't understand.

Lack of motivation to succeed in school can cause inattention and acting out. Every year Robert's teachers say the same thing, that he is just not working up to his ability. He doesn't seem to care. Robert sits in class and talks to others, fools around, and disrupts the class, but he doesn't pay attention or complete assignments. Homework is never done, and when it is completed it usually contains numerous mistakes. Robert's teachers send notes home almost every other day, but they never hear from his parents. It seems that his parents don't care whether Robert receives a good education or not.

American Academy of Pediatrics Guidelines for Assessment of ADHD

In 2000, the American Academy of Pediatrics (AAP) published guidelines for doing an assessment of ADHD. Among its recommendations were the following.
1. The primary care clinician should initiate an evaluation of children ages six to twelve who present with inattention, hyperactivity, or impulsivity.
2. The diagnosis of ADHD requires that a child meet the DSM-IV criteria.
3. The assessment requires evidence directly obtained from parents or caregivers regarding the core symptoms of ADHD in various settings, the age of onset of symptoms, duration of symptoms, and the degree of functional impairment.
4. The assessment of ADHD requires evidence directly obtained from the classroom teacher (or other school professional).
5. The assessment should include evaluation for associated conditions.
6. Other diagnostic tests are not routinely indicated to establish a diagnosis of ADHD but may be used for the assessment of co-existing conditions (e.g., learning disabilities, mental retardation).

The AAP recommended that specific questionnaires and rating scales that have been developed to assess the behavioral characteristics of ADHD be used in the assessment process. Furthermore, the AAP recognized that the child's classroom teacher typically has more information about the child's behavior than other professionals at the school and should be contacted to provide information about the child. This information can be obtained through narrative reports (oral or written), questionnaires, or rating scales and any reports should focus on the presence of the core symptoms of ADHD. Furthermore, for children who are educated in their homes by parents, evidence of the presence of core symptoms in settings other than the home should be obtained. When a child spends considerable time in other structured settings (i.e., after-school care) additional information should be sought from professionals in those settings.

The evaluator should consider the possible presence of co-existing conditions. This may include conditions such as parent-child interaction problems, motor disabilities, speech and language disorders, oppositional disorder, conduct disorder, learning problems, anxiety disorder, depression, etc. The child may be referred to specialists in these areas for more comprehensive assessment.

According to the AAP, other diagnostic tests such as thyroid function tests, brain imaging studies, electroencephalography, and continuous performance tests contribute little to establishing the diagnosis of ADHD.

Members of the ADHD Assessment Team

While the AAP guidelines were written for primary care physicians, often other health care professionals and care givers are involved in the assessment process. For parents who are seeking an evaluation, it is best to find professionals who are knowledgeable about ADHD and who have experience evaluating and treating those with ADHD. Physicians, clinical psychologists, school psychologists, clinical social workers, speech-language pathologists, learning specialists, audiologists, occupational therapists, and educators may each play an important role in the ADHD assessment team.

The Physician
The child's pediatrician or family physician is often the first person parents talk to when they suspect their child is having a problem. The physician, usually familiar with the child's medical history and already having some knowledge of the family through previous treatment contact, is in a good position to help.. However, depending on what the doctor says, the assessment process may begin or end with this first request for help. It is important to make sure the physician has a good understanding of the symptoms your child exhibits both at home and at school, the length of time these symptoms have existed, and the problems they are causing to your child and to others. Bring some documentation from the school with you that illustrates these problems and, if possible, have the teacher complete a simple ADHD symptom checklist and bring it with you to the office visit.

Primary care physicians, psychiatrists, and neurologists will start by taking a medical and social history. When possible, both parents should be present to provide the doctor with information. The history may alert the doctor to health problems which could account for the development of ADHD symptoms. Information about the pregnancy and delivery including maternal health during pregnancy, use of alcohol, smoking, toxemia or eclampsia, postmaturity of the fetus, and extended labor should be reviewed. Detailed information about the early development of the child, educational progress, and behavior at home, at school, and within the community are essential parts of the history. Furthermore, the doctor should collect information about family relationships paying particular concern to any stresses on the child that could affect behavior and performance.

Routine physical examinations of children with ADHD are often normal, nevertheless they are necessary to rule out the unlikely possibility of there being another medical illness that could cause ADHD-like symptoms. Vision or hearing deficits should be ruled out. The physician should look out for other medical conditions that might predispose the child to ADHD including fragile X syndrome, fetal alcohol syndrome, and phenylketonuria. Tests such as chromosome studies, magnetic resonance imaging (MRI), or computerized axial tomograms (CAT scans) are not to be used routinely for evaluation of ADHD. However, there is a small, but growing, body of research that is demonstrating that ADHD may be accurately assessed using quantitative EEG (QEEG) data. This classification technique is based on the observation of distinct measurable changes that ADHD patients exhibit in their brain wave activity relative to normal subjects. The electrical activity of the child's brainwave activity is measured via a collection method called an electroencephalography or EEG.

Psychiatrists and neurologists, trained in the assessment and treatment of ADHD and other neurological and psychiatric disorders, play an important part in identifying ADHD as well as other possible related conditions such as learning disabilities, Tourette's syndrome, pervasive developmental disorder, obsessive compulsive disorder, anxiety disorder, depression, or bipolar disorder. Children who have co-existing conditions and those who do not respond well to standard medication therapies may benefit from consulting a specialist.

The Clinical or School Psychologist

The clinical or school psychologist administers and interprets psychological and educational tests of cognition, perception, and language development (such as intelligence, attention span, visual-motor skills, memory, impulsivity), as well as tests of achievement and social/emotional adjustment. Results of such tests provide important clues as to whether a person's difficulties are related to ADHD and/or other problems with learning, behavior, or emotional adjustment. Psychologists and other mental health professionals often integrate data collected from parents and teachers who complete behavior rating scales about the child. Most of the rating scales used to assess ADHD provide standardized scores on a number of factors, usually related to attention span, self-control, learning ability, hyperactivity, aggression, social behavior, and anxiety. Remember, there is no test for ADHD. Even though psychological and educational testing can give you a better picture of the child's strengths and weaknesses, satisfactory performance on these tests does not rule out ADHD.

The Child's School

Public schools are required by federal law to evaluate students suspected of having a disability. The Individuals with Disabilities in Education Act (IDEA 2004) requires schools to follow specific procedures and standards to perform such evaluations. Frequently, the evaluation process is either initiated by the teacher or the parent. A child study team, made up of school personnel such as the guidance counselor, a learning specialist, the principal or his designee, one or more of the student's teachers, or others at the school, will meet to discuss the student. As a first step in the assessment process, the child study team will collect information about the student from his parents and teachers. If this information indicates that the student is showing signs of a disability, further assessment may be done by the school psychologist and other school professionals. Assessments should always include information about the student's current and past classroom performance, academic skill strengths and weaknesses, attention span, and other social, emotional, and behavioral characteristics. Such information can be gathered through teacher interviews, review of cumulative records, analysis of test scores, and direct observation of the student in class. Assessment data enables the school to determine the needs of the student. The student may be eligible for special education and related services or for a 504 Plan that provides accommodations in the regular classroom.

The Family and Child

Having witnessed the child in a variety of situations over a number of years, parents have a unique perspective on the child's previous development and current adjustment. This information is usually acquired by interview and through questionnaires. The parent also plays an important role in driving the assessment process so that no unnecessary delays occur and that the child receives a thorough assessment by qualified professionals. If there is any doubt that an appropriate assessment was done, the parent should speak to the professionals involved. Get a second opinion if you are unsure of the findings.

An interview with the child offers the clinician an opportunity to observe the child's cognitive functioning and behavior first-hand and can yield valuable information about his social and emotional adjustment, feelings about himself and others, and attitudes about school and other aspects of daily life. Observations of the child's behavior during interviews, such as his level of activity, attentiveness, or compliance, should not be noted as typical of his behavior in other settings. Normal behavior in a one-on-one setting does not diminish the likelihood of the child having ADHD.

Procedures Used in Doing an Assessment of ADHD

Behavior Rating Scales

Rating scales have been developed over the past thirty-five years to assess general child psychopathology and others have focused on assessing symptoms of ADHD and related disorders. Behavior rating scales can offer valid and reliable information about a child, thus providing a means by which to compare a child's behavior to that of others of the same age and sex. Many of the scales used to assess ADHD focus very heavily on a number of factors, usually related to attention span, self-control, learning ability, hyperactivity, aggression, social behavior, anxiety, etc. Most of these rating scales have parallel versions for parents and teachers. Some rating scales have versions for children to self-report. The advantage of rating scales with parallel parent, teacher, and self-report versions is that the scores across the different informants can be compared.

Earlier scales developed in the 1960's and 1970's were normed on small samples and lacked rigorous standardization. Newer scales provide superior measures because they utilize a broader pool of items, employ newer rating formats, and are developed on larger samples of subjects, therefore resulting in better standardization.

One of the best advantages of rating scales, as compared to interviews, is that they are easy to administer and inexpensive. Time for administration is usually modest. They can be sent by mail or electronically or can be answered over a telephone. They provide a standard set of behaviors to be evaluated, thereby reducing variability in the information that is obtained about the child and ensuring that specific target behaviors will be assessed. They offer a means by which to evaluate the frequency and severity of specific behaviors and provide age and sex-graded norms to determine whether reported behaviors are appropriate or deviant in relation to normal peers. Rater bias and subjectivity of responding is reduced by using a standardized presentation of questions. They can be routinely administered in health settings and schools, and many rating scales have good data on reliability and validity.

Rating scales also have a number of disadvantages. They are limited to the informant's perspective. Information that may be relevant to the subject, but that is not covered by the items of the scale will be missed. With rating scales alone, it is not possible to explore the informant's responses and subjective experiences, nor is it possible to observe behavior directly. Rating scales can be subject to rater bias based upon the characteristics of the rater. For example, mothers who are depressed rate their children as having greater behavior problems than those who are not depressed. Slight changes in the wording of instructions, or the wording of the items themselves, may have a significant effect on the informant's response. Data obtained from ratings rely totally on the rater's familiarity with the child and, to some extent, upon the rater's familiarity with normative behavior of other children of the same age and sex. Thus, elementary school teachers, who spend several hours a day with a student, for example, may be more familiar with the student's behavior than a middle or high school teacher whose contact with the student is limited to one period per day. Therefore, in secondary education settings, it is essential to receive ratings from several teachers so as to accurately assess behavior throughout the day. Rating scales are also subject to rater bias based upon other characteristics of the child. Likeable children may be rated less negatively on scales of hyperactivity and inattention than aggressive/stubborn children.

Despite these shortcomings, behavior rating scales can offer important information that can be helpful in the assessment process. Below are a list of rating scales that are commonly used in the assessment process for ADHD.

- ADD-H Comprehensive Teacher Rating Scale (ACTeRS)
- ADHD Rating Scale
- BASC-2: Behavior Assessment System for Children, Second Edition
- Behavior Rating Inventory of Executive Function (BRIEF)
- Brown Attention-Deficit Disorder Scales
- Child Behavior Checklist (CBCL-Teacher)
- Child Attention Profile (CAP)
- Child Symptom Inventories (CSI)
- Conners Teacher and Parent Rating Scales-Revised
- Home Situations Questionnaire
- IOWA-Conners Rating Scale
- School Situations Questionnaire
- SNAP-IV Rating Scale and SNAP-IV-C Rating Scale
- Vanderbilt Assessment Scale (Teacher Informant and Parent Informant)

Psychometric Testing

For many children suspected of having ADHD, psychometric testing is an important and necessary part of a diagnostic assessment. Data relevant to a child's intellectual ability, information processing skills, and academic achievement is obtained through psychometric testing. This information is helpful in understanding the child's learning style, whether or not there are any signs of a learning disability, or if there are academic achievement deficits.

Psychometric testing may involve evaluating intellectual ability, attention span, visual-motor skills, paired-associate learning, impulsivity, short-term memory, and a number of other cognitive functions. Tests are frequently administered by a clinical, school, or educational psychologist who is trained to administer them and interpret the results. Test findings are usually communicated in a written report that outlines information about the child's presenting problems, the developmental and social history, the test data, interpretation of the test results in terms of specific strengths and weaknesses of the child, and recommendations for interventions when necessary.

Intelligence testing. Intelligence testing is frequently done to obtain an overall measure of the child's intellectual ability. The two tests that are used most often for this purpose are: Wechsler Preschool and Primary Scale of Intelligence-Third Edition (WPPSI-III) and the Wechsler Intelligence Scale for Children-Fourth Edition (WISC-IV).

Neuropsychological testing. Neuropsychological test batteries evaluate strengths and weaknesses of cognitive function. The NEPSY (Korkman et al., 1997), for example, includes scores for language and communication, sensorimotor functions, visual-spatial abilities, learning and memory, and executive functions such as attention and planning. The most common neuropsychological functions assessed are: language, memory, visual-spatial skills, attention, executive functioning, motor abilities, and adaptive function.

Executive functioning. Some tests have been developed to measure the high-level functions of planning, inhibiting immediate or inappropriate reactions, decision-making, and organization. For the most part their standardization is weak. "Executive function" is a weakly defined concept, therefore, tests that have been designed to measure different aspects of this concept have had difficulty doing so.

Motor abilities and adaptive function. Children can have significant difficulties with organization and coordination of motor tasks. With a clinical neurological examination, patterns of incoordination can be determined as well as underlying causes (such as mild cerebral palsy). There are standardized tests available to quantify levels of incoordination more precisely. Scales have also been developed that include items relating to self-care and independence skills. Quantifying these kinds of "adaptive functions" are important in assessing the needs of children with global learning disabilities. The Vineland Adaptive Behavior Scales (Sparrow et al., 1984) are widely used for this purpose and have a practical advantage in that information can be acquired by parental report as well as by direct examination of the child's abilities.

Achievement Tests. Tests of academic achievement are routinely incorporated in assessments of school-age children. Since many of the problems of children with ADHD are school related, and since a significant number (about twenty-five percent) of ADHD children also have a co-existing learning disability, it is important to examine the child's achievement skills to assess weaknesses in areas of reading, arithmetic, and written language. Standardized tests used for this purpose include such instruments as: Woodcock-Johnson Psychoeducational Test Battery: Tests of Achievement, the Wechsler Individual Achievement Test, (WIAT), Wide Range Achievement Test (WRAT-R), Test of Written Language (TOWL), Kaufman ABC (K-ABC), Woodcock Reading Mastery Test, Key Math, and others.

Social and emotional development. Assessment procedures to evaluate social and emotional development include: structured approaches to diagnostic interviewing; use of standardized measures including inventories and rating scales that are completed by parents and teachers and self-report; observation of the child; and other forms of testing. The structured interview is the most often used procedure for assessment of social and emotional functioning and development in children. The collection of information through the interview in a coherent, structured fashion provides valuable facts to the clinician. Interviews are often held with multiple informants (caregivers, other family members, teachers, and the child in question, etc). Observations of behavior play a central role in helping clinicians evaluate social and emotional development. Observations may begin in the waiting room, while the child is being interviewed, during administration of psychological tests, in the classroom, or in less structured social settings. Standardized inventories and rating scales with parent and teacher informants and self-report are also useful tools in an assessment of social and emotional development of the child.

Continuous Performance Tests. Computerized assessment of attention span and the ability to inhibit responding has been used for more than thirty years in laboratories doing research on hyperactive children. These tests, called continuous performance tests (CPT), can be either visual or auditory and require the child to attend to a screen and selectively respond to a specific stimulus (i.e., letters, numbers, geometric figures, objects, sounds, etc.) and not respond to others. Many years of research indicated that children with ADHD tend to do less well on such tasks. Some of the more common CPTs used in clinical practice are: Conners Continuous Performance Test II, Tests of Variables of Attention (TOVA), Gordon Diagnostic System, and the Integrated Visual and Auditory Continuous Performance Test (IVA). Some professionals believe CPTs provide objective information about an individual's ability to maintain attention and control impulsive responding. While there is support for the use of such tests, there is also controversy among professionals about the value of CPTs in the assessment of ADHD. Everyone agrees that they should never be the sole measure a clinician uses in an assessment.

After the Assessment

Ideally, after all the data has been collected, members of the assessment team should collaborate to discuss their findings. In private, community-based assessments, such collaboration is usually done through phone calls from one professional to another or by sending reports of findings. Rarely do all the members of the community-based assessment team meet together with the parents and child (if appropriate) to discuss their findings. In school-based assessments, members of the assessment team usually do come together with the parents and child (if appropriate) to discuss their findings.

Ideally, assessment data should lead to a thorough understanding of the child's strengths and areas of need physically, academically, behaviorally, and emotionally. If a diagnosis of ADHD and/or other disorders is made, treatment planning should include all areas where interventions are recommended. The physician may discuss appropriate medical interventions. The psychologist or other mental health professionals may discuss counseling, behavior modification, or social and study skills training options. The school may set up classroom interventions to accommodate the child's areas of need in school or may provide special education or related services. Some or all members of the assessment team may become part of the treatment team, which is responsible for managing the treatment of the child.

Once the initial assessment is completed and appropriate treatment is instituted, there should be routine follow-up by members of the team to determine how the child is progressing. ADHD, which is a chronic condition, will often require long-term care and monitoring on a regular basis. Parents play a key role in monitoring treatment effectiveness and in encouraging members of the treatment team to collaborate with one another when making decisions.

Evaluating children for ADHD can be a time-consuming process. Get copies of all the evaluations and treatment recommendations made by the professionals involved. Maintain these records because you may need to provide them to other professionals or to schools in the future. Coordination of this information and services, whether it be by you or a professional on your child's team, is no simple task, but the outcome is usually well worth the effort.

Summary

The evaluation of a child for ADHD usually involves more than one professional. Physicians, psychologists, educators, and others may be part of the assessment team responsible for the evaluation. Information about your child's history and current functioning will be obtained from you, your son or daughter (when possible), and from past and current teachers. This information may be collected through interviews, completion of standardized scales, psychological or educational testing, direct observation of the child in school, and review of school and health records.

Findings from the assessment should lead to a diagnosis. If ADHD or another condition is diagnosed, appropriate treatments and interventions should be recommended. Some or all of the members of the assessment team may stay involved as providers of treatment. Parents often have the time-consuming task of monitoring the progress of their child and informing members of the treatment team about the effectiveness of specific interventions.

Chapter 6   Parenting Strategies to Manage Behavior

In a perfect world children would always do what they are told. Unfortunately, the world is not perfect and no one I know has a perfectly well-behaved child. The truth is that no child obeys parental commands or follows rules even close to one hundred percent of the time. In fact, about half of all families of children who are four to seven years of age report disobedience at home to be a problem and noncompliance is a frequent reason why parents seek mental health services.

Children with ADHD, especially the hyperactive-impulsive and combined types, have a greater risk of developing noncompliant behavior. Such children, by definition, have difficulty inhibiting behavior, paying attention to their surroundings, and following through on parental commands, particularly when the command prevents them from doing what they want. They have difficulty making transitions from doing what they like to something they like less. They become easily frustrated and readily show dissatisfaction. They have trouble waiting, planning, and forseeing consequences to their behavior and thus they are often "managed by the moment" rather than by reason. Dr. Russell Barkley has indicated that children with ADHD have a deficit in rule-governed behavior that may cause them not to listen and fail to follow instructions and stick to a task.

What Factors Contribute to Childhood Noncompliance

By ages two and three, most children should already be able to understand commands given by their parents and teachers and they possess the physical ability and self-control necessary to carry them out. As their ability to comply increases so does their desire for autonomy and so they become less willing to comply. However, as they go through early childhood, children generally become more cooperative. By the start of elementary school they are able to handle the increasing social demands that will be placed on them and should have little trouble complying.

Some children, however, do not follow this path of compliance and, instead, become more and more noncompliant. What are the factors that contribute to this? Hyperactivity is one. Temperament is another. Some children seem to be born with temperaments that predispose them to develop behavior problems. From very early in life, these children are intense, negative, and non-adaptable. Difficult temperament may cause parents to adopt coercive styles of interaction with the child that could worsen behavior and affect the quality of the parent-child relationship. Types of parenting practices that have been associated with the development of noncompliance in children include inconsistent discipline, irritable explosive discipline, little supervision of child behavior, low levels of involvement with the child, and inflexible and rigid parenting styles.

Also contributing to noncompliance is a pattern in families of negatively reinforcing the child who disobeys by removing a punishment or providing a reward or privilege after the child acts out inappropriately. For example, a mother tells a child he cannot watch televison until his homework is completed, but then backs down and allows the child to watch after he throws a tantrum or argues, thereby reinforcing the noncompliant behavior.

Rex Forehand and Robert McMahon address these issues in their book, *Helping the Noncompliant Child*, which is a text for professionals who are interested in teaching parent training programs. This chapter summarizes the main points of their program and reviews other parent training programs.

Types of Parent Training Programs

Traditional parent training programs have common features in that they teach parents skills related to attending, rewarding, ignoring, instructing, and the use of time-out. The programs make use of home practice assignments and exercises and use direct instruction and modeling as primary teaching methods. One of the best known of these traditional parent training programs is Russell Barkley's *Defiant Children*, which is suitable for children up to the age of twelve. In addition to the skills noted above, Barkley has incorporated a number of additional components to teach parents, including information specific to ADHD, a token reinforcement system, and a daily report card system for school problems.

Another well-known and widely used program for children between two and twelve years of age is Tom Phelan's *1-2-3 Magic*. This program focuses on the use of time-out as a consequence for noncompliance and teaches parents the appropriate ways to administer time-out and correct misbehavior.

Ross Greene has developed a program for difficult children who display noncompliance accompanied by angry and explosive behavior. Greene calls his approach Collaborative Problem

Solving (CPS), and he describes it in detail in his best-selling book, *The Explosive Child*.

In their book, *Try and Make Me*, Ray Levy and Bill O'Hanlon teach parents to use an approach they call "Practice Academy" to manage noncompliant behavior. This approach incorporates the behavioral strategy referred to as "overcorrection" in an effort to teach the noncompliant child appropriate behavior. The Practice Academy approach contains four simple steps for parents to apply to correct misbehavior.

The remainder of this chapter will focus on these training programs. You can choose which ones you think are best suited for you and your child or take ideas from all of them to incorporate in your discipline program at home.

Traditional Parent Training

Most traditional approaches to parent training teach a similar set of skills to be used by parents of noncompliant children to improve behavior and compliance. These skills can be summarized as follows: increasing parental attention and positive reinforcement to the child for engaging in socially appropriate and compliant behavior; reducing any positive reinforcement (such as parental attention) being provided to the child for engaging in disruptive or defiant behavior; and applying punishment when the child exhibits inappropriate or noncompliant behavior. In most programs, positive reinforcement may involve parental attention, snacks, toys, privileges, or tokens that can be exchanged for privileges and toys. Punishment usually takes the form of time-out, but it can also include loss of privileges or tokens. In addition, parents are provided with guidelines to clearly give instructions and in the use of home token economy programs and daily report cards for use in school. This chapter will help you learn and practice the skills taught in traditional parent training programs.

Skill 1: Using Positive Reinforcement to Strengthen Appropriate Behavior

Attention and rewards are two types of positive reinforcement that parents can use to strengthen appropriate behavior.

People, in general, and children, in particular, respond better to praise than punishment or disinterest. Often, as parents we tend to take our children's positive behavior for granted and we fail to attend to, or positively reinforce, appropriate behavior. When a behavior is followed by a reinforcer (verbal praise, a smile, a hug, or a reward of some sort), that behavior is strengthened, and it is more likely to be repeated in the future. Our failure to recognize, praise, or reward the child often enough for doing the right thing is a very common mistake that can lead to a weakening of appropriate behavior. Frequent positive reinforcement not only increases the probability of a behavior being repeated, but it also helps the child feel good, builds confidence, and provides encouragement and motivation.

The practice of using positive reinforcement to change the behavior of a child is easy to understand, however, few people do it well. Some parents just find it very hard to give compliments. They withhold their approval, offering praise and congratulations only for outstanding accomplishments. Such parents fail to realize the powerful benefits of a few kind words delivered consistently. At the opposite extreme, other parents offer positive reinforcement too liberally. They literally gush with praise, hugs, and other displays of affection no matter what the child does. Parents who are interested in changing behavior should provide positive reinforcement contingent on the child displaying the behavior that the parent would like to see increased.

When teaching a new behavior, it is best to reinforce every time the behavior occurs. New behaviors require immediate and continuous reinforcement in order to get started. For more complicated behaviors (i.e., completing homework before dinner), it is important to reinforce in small steps. This is called shaping. For example, to shape your child to pay attention to homework it would be important to provide positive reinforcement at several points in the process of homework completion. In this example, reinforcement could be given for writing the complete homework assignment down in school, for bringing home the proper books, for getting down to work at the correct time, and while the child is actually doing the homework. Such immediate and continuous reinforcement in small steps is better than a parent just complimenting the child after all of the homework is completed.

Physical reinforcers such as privileges, food, refreshments, money, toys, or tokens, among others, are useful in changing behavior. Some parents are hesitant to offer such reinforcers as they feel that they are bribing their child to behave appropriately. Keep in mind that we all work for physical reinforcers (money usually) and that bribes usually refer to payment that one gets for doing something inappropriate or illegal.

Children with ADHD need to be reinforced more frequently than other children. They may also benefit from written contracts, point programs, sticker charts. or other tangible programs that provide tokens that can be exchanged for privileges and rewards. These will be discussed later.

At this time, please complete the worksheet on the next page to review the use of positive reinforcement to manage behavior (additional copies of this and other worksheets are in the Appendix).

Using Positive Reinforcement Worksheet

This worksheet is designed to help parents recognize how they have been using positive reinforcement to manage their child's misbehavior and to practice doing so.

Step 1: Think Positive
List several ways in which you provide positive reinforcement to your child for behaving appropriately. Put a check mark next to the reinforcers that you think are most effective in strengthening your child's positive behavior.
A. Example: Verbal praise such as "You're a great listener."
B. Example: Bragging to others about the child in earshot of the child.

1. _____
2. _____
3. _____
4. _____
5. _____

Step 2: Identify Two Target Behavior To Reinforce
Fill in the item below with two target behaviors that you would like your child to exhibit more often (as in the example below).
Target Behavior to Reinforce:
A. Example: Sitting down and doing homework by himself in room and working for twenty minutes.

1. _____
2. _____

Step 3: Plan Your Reinforcement
Write down exactly how you plan to reinforce your child each time the target behaviors listed above are done.
Everytime my child _____
I will reinforce him/her by_____

Step 4: Reinforce Immediately and Continuously
When strengthening a new behavior it is best at first to reinforce immediately and frequently. Remind yourself to look for the target behavior or behavior that resembles the target behavior and immediately deliver the reinforcement. Catch the child being good.

Step 5: Keep Track of Your Child's Success
Create a chart at home for the target behavior you want your child to exhibit more often and provide stickers, happy faces, etc., as reinforcement. Provide an incentive for good performance on the chart.

Skill 2: Ignore Inappropriate Behavior

While positive reinforcement strengthen's behavior, ignoring negative behavior can weaken it.

Ignoring can have a powerful influence on behavior, particularly those behaviors that are attention-seeking in nature (e.g., whining, nagging, temper tantrums, interruptions). These behaviors tend to decrease when the child does not receive attention for them.

Many children with ADHD will have a more severe reaction when parents ignore their misbehavior. They may yell to get the parent's attention. Parents will have to remain more steadfast in ignoring this behavior than may otherwise be required for non-ADHD children. When it gets to be too much the parent may have to go to another room (reverse time-out) for a short while.

Keep these rules for ignoring in mind:
1. Ignoring works best for attention-seeking behaviors (e.g., whining, nagging, temper tantrums, interrupting). Behaviors that are potentially destructive or harmful to people or property (e.g., fighting, name calling, throwing something) should not be ignored. The parent can intervene by stopping the behavior and using time-out.
2. Identify your child's specific behavior that you plan to ignore.
3. Explain ahead of time to your child that you are going to ignore certain behaviors that you find inappropriate (e.g., "Jimmy, I am going to ignore you when you .... I am going to turn away and not look at you or talk to you. When I do this it means I don't like what you are doing. When you stop, I will stop ignoring you.")
4. When ignoring the child, do not make eye contact with him. It is best to turn away from him so that no eye contact is possible. This gives a very clear message to the child that the parent is actively ignoring the behavior.
5. When ignoring the child, do not talk to him. Do not offer any explanation to him about his behavior and do not answer questions from him. The appropriate time to provide an explanation for ignoring is when he is behaving appropriately.
6. Do not have any physical contact with him. When you start ignoring him, he may tug or your clothes, sit on your lap, or become aggressive. If this happens, try standing when ignoring him as these contact behaviors are less likely to occur and it also sends a message to him that you are actively ignoring the behavior. If he continues to speak or touch you in response to your ignoring you may have to leave the room (kind of a reverse time-out) to avoid paying attention and reinforcing his behavior.
7. Start ignoring when the inappropriate behavior begins. Stop ignoring ten to fifteen seconds after the inappropriate behavior ends.
8. Ignore the inappropriate behavior at all times.
9. Positively reinforce appropriate behavior by providing attention or rewards.

Skill 3: Listening Practice

Listening practice is for children under the age of nine. It is designed to positively reinforce the child for correctly listening to commands. When the child complies with the command, the parent positively reinforces his compliance. However, if the child refuses to comply, the parent is then to warn the child that he will have to go to time-out. Further noncompliance will result in time-out (read the next section on using time-out).

For the next two weeks, spend five to ten minutes each day and explain to your child that this time will be used for Listening Practice. During Listening Practice, make sure that your child has your undivided attention. Proceed to give several simple assertive commands to the child followed by positive verbal reinforcement for listening.

For example:
Parent says: "Johnny, please close your bedroom door." If the child complies, praise and give another command (e.g., "You're a good listener. Now, please put your shoes in your room.") If the child complies, once again praise and issue another command. If the child refuses to comply, issue a warning that the child will have to go to time-out unless he complies. If the child continues not to comply, follow through with time-out. If the child listens to the command praise his compliance and issue another command. Continue until you are finished issuing about seven to ten commands.

Please remember that the purpose of Listening Practice is to teach your child to follow instructions. Keep these practice sessions positive and fun. Try to make a game out of listening and take a few minutes each day to practice the listening exercise.

Skill 4: Giving Clear Instructions

In their book, *Helping the Noncompliant Child*, Robert McMahon and Rex Forehand stress the importance of giving clear instructions to the child to reduce noncompliant behavior. They point out that clear instructions are necessary when it is important to the parent that the child do something immediately; when the parent is not willing to offer a choice of behaviors to the child, but insists on a specific behavior; or if the child is behaving in a way that might possibly harm themselves, other people, or property.

Providing clear, specific instructions improves the likelihood of compliance. McMahon and Forehand describe a few general types of unclear instructions that can lower the rate of child compliance. I added a few more.

Type of Unclear Instruction	Examples
Chain commands	Put your plate in the sink, rinse it off, put it in the dishwasher, and bring me the napkins.

Vague commands	Be careful. Watch out. Act your age. Be a good boy (girl).
Question commands	Would you like to take out the trash?
"Let's ..." commands	Let's go clean up your room.
Commands followed by a rationale or other verbalization	Please pick up the toys in here. (Child asks why). Because your mother's boss is coming for dinner tonight, and we want the house to look nice.
Aggressive, threatening commands	Clean your toys now or you will go to bed early.
Nagging commands	Clean your toys. Clean your toys. Clean your toys.
Commands from a distance	(Parent is in another room and yells to the child.) Take your bath and get ready for bed.

The problem with chain commands is that they may result in information overload, particularly if your child has ADHD and has problems with working memory. You may be setting your child up to fail to comply.

Vague commands do not provide enough detail for the child. The vague command assumes the child knows what the parent wants, but this may not be the case. Noncompliant children generally respond better to precise commands. These are very specific and spell out the parents expectations exactly. The child is told what to do, when, and how (if necessary).

Question commands can be the most problematic as they do not signal that the parent is in charge. Parents should not ask commands. For example, "Would you like to do your homework after dinner?" This gives the child the option to say no. When the parent expects compliance with a command, it should be direct and made in the form of an imperative statement and not a question.

The problem with "Let's" commands is that they imply that the parent shares the responsibility of carrying out the command (e.g., "Let's clean your room."). If the parent intends to help the child then this type of command is appropriate. However, the parent who has no intention of helping the child, but who thinks that this may be a softer, gentler way to approach the child, may be mistaken. The child may feel tricked and noncompliance could be increased.

Commands should not be followed by a rationale or other explanation. Any such rationale or explanation should precede the command. For example, "We are expecting company tonight so pick up the toys in the family room." When the rationale follows the command, the directive is obscured or the child is given an opportunity for rebuttal. The result is that the child is less likely to comply. Remember that one of the biggest mistakes parents make is to talk too much after giving a command.

Aggressive or threatening commands do not create a positive atmosphere for compliance. Some noncompliant children will take offense to the hostile tone of these types of commands and you will create unnecessary defiance. Commands work best if they are clear, specific, and authoritative, but connote respect for the child.

Nagging commands are those that parents repeat over and over. The child has not complied the first time the command was given so the parent just continues to repeat it. The child learns not to comply until the parent raises his/her voice, makes a threat, or comes closer to the child to make sure the command is carried out. These types of commands teach the child not to listen the first time they are told to do something. The child learns that the parent will repeat the command many more times before they will take action.

Commands given from a distance have less likelihood of being followed than commands given near the child. When parents are out of sight of the child, they have no idea if the child followed the command. Often, the child will delay until the parent comes into the room and states the command again.

Practice Giving Clear Instructions Worksheet

Follow these steps when giving a command.
1. Get the child's attention.
2. Move close to the child.
3. Say the child's name.
4. Establish eye contact.
5. State the command clearly in a firm voice.
6. Use a "do" command rather than a "stop" command when you can. For example, "Please put the game away now!" versus "Stop fooling around!"
7. Provide any explanation before stating the command, not after.
8. Wait five seconds.
9. Do not talk to the child during this time.
10. Do not walk away or look away.

If the child starts to comply:
1. Pay attention as the child begins to execute the command.
2. Praise or reward the child when the command has been performed correctly.

If the child does not begin to comply within 5 seconds.
1. Issue a warning as an "If...then" statement that specifies the desired behavior and the consequences for noncompliance (e.g., "If you don't put away the game, then you will have to go to time-out."
2. Allow five more seconds for compliance.
3. If the child complies the parent continues to pay attention and provides praise.
4. If the child does not comply the parent follows through on the previous warning.

Skill # 4: Using Time-out

Time-out is a very effective procedure to use in managing misbehavior. Simply put, time-out means that the child is removed from a reinforcing situation and is instructed to spend time in a dull, non-reinforcing environment. Time-out can result in rapid behavioral change. Some misbehaviors will decrease if the parents ignore the misbehavior. However, for highly annoying misbehaviors such as sibling rivalry, temper tantrums, or aggressive and destructive behavior, ignoring takes too long to produce behavioral change and it is unlikely that most parents would have the patience to ignore such misbehavior for very long.

Step 1. Identify those misbehaviors for which you will use a time-out punishment. Use the space in the following worksheet to list specific misbehaviors to time-out and alternative appropriate behaviors to reinforce. Remember, whenever you use a punishment program to change misbehavior, it is important that you also institute a reinforcement program to encourage more positive behavior.

Step 2. Decide on a time-out location. Since time-out, by definition, requires a nonreinforcing environment, you should pick a place in the house where there are no toys, games, televisions, books, or people. The child's room may not be a good place to use for time-out because of all the distractions available to the child. Some parents prefer to use a time-out chair placed in a quiet room and instruct the child to sit in the chair. Other places for time out may include steps on a staircase, a bathroom (all medications and sharp tools should be removed), or a spare room that does not contain toys, televisions, video games, or other enjoyable activities.

Step 3. Decide on the appropriate length of the punishment. A good rule of thumb to use is one minute of time-out per year of age of the child for mild misbehavior and two minutes per year of age for more serious misbehavior. This may be shortened to a half-minute per year of age for children with ADHD who have great difficulty sitting still. It is very helpful to use a portable timer with a bell or buzzer to signal the end of a time-out period. For children with ADHD, parents are encouraged to ignore minor motor movements of the child while he is in the time-out chair or for those who just cannot sit in the chair, the parent may put a border of masking tape around the chair giving the child some leeway in moving around without being penalized.

Step 4. Instruct the child to go to time-out and enforcing the time-out punishment. Since the purpose of using time-out is to replace more aggressive, negative, and/or emotional forms of punishment such as yelling, scolding, and spanking, it is important that instructions to go to time-out be given to the child in an unemotional way, using firm and assertive commands. The parent should avoid lecturing, name calling, arguing, or asking rhetorical questions such as "How many times do I have to tell you not to do that?" or "When are you going to listen?" This only serves to provide more attention to the child for his misbehavior and may inadvertently reinforce the undesirable behavior.

For example, after observing the child teasing his baby sister the parent should say:

"Mark, stop teasing your sister or you will go to time-out."

The parent should then count silently to five. If the child has stopped teasing, the parent should reinforce him for listening. If the child continues to tease, the parent should walk over to the child, make eye contact, and assertively say:

"Mark, if you do not stop teasing your sister, you will go to time-out."

If the child does not comply, the parent should escort the child to the time-out place, set the timer for the correct number of minutes, and instruct the child to stay there and think about what he did wrong until the timer goes off. After completing time-out, the child is required to state what he did wrong and apologize. In situations where time-out was used because the child did not do something that was asked of him (e.g., brushing his teeth) the child is instructed to brush after the time-out period is completed. Refusal to do so is followed by another time-out.

Not all children respond to time-out cooperatively. Some children resist going to time-out from the start and will aggressively test the limits of the program. Many children do this by arguing with the parent to see if they can successfully persuade the parent not to enforce time-out. Children are quite skilled at doing this and employ all sorts of tactics, such as promising never to misbehave like that again, blaming their misbehavior on someone else, or denying that they ever misbehaved in the first place. Ignore these excuses and promises and follow through with time-out. By giving in to the child's manipulations the parent loses credibility, making it only that much more difficult to enforce time-out with the child in the future.

Some children use more aggressive tactics than just verbal persuasion and excuses to avoid going to time-out. In some cases a child will physically resist being placed in time-out. When this happens the parent may have to hold the child's hand and walk him to time-out. With young children, the parent may have to carry the child to time-out.

Another problem may arise once the child is placed in time-out. Some children will tantrum, scream, or threaten to leave time-out prematurely. In such cases the parent must firmly remind the child that time-out will not start until he is quiet. If the child is sent to time-out in a separate room and keeps coming out, the parent may have to close the door and leave it closed until the child calms down (usually just for less than one minute). Once calm, the parent can open the door. If the child tries to leave, the parent may have to hold the door closed or put a lock on the outside of the door to keep the door locked for a minute or two. The parent could offer to open or unlock the door if the child agrees to stay in time-out quietly with the door open. If neither alternative is possible, the parent may have to use backup consequences such as the removal of additional privileges (e.g., television time, playtime outside) until time-out is served.

For young children, the parent may hold the child in their lap while sitting in the time-out chair. This is to be done without speaking to the child or giving the child any attention whatsoever. The purpose of this holding is merely to restrain the child in time-out. Usually children dislike being confined in an adult's lap, and, after a few times of testing the limits, the child will give up the struggle to get out of serving the time-out and will comply more willingly.

Time-out can be an effective method of punishment for managing misbehavior. However, for it to work, it must be used properly. Remember, it takes time for the child to realize that mom and dad mean it when they say to go to time-out.

To summarize, below are the points you should remember when you use time-out.

- Warn the child to listen or to stop misbehaving just one or two times before giving a time-out.
- Send the child to time-out if the warning is ignored.
- Ignore the child if he tries to talk you out of using time-out.
- Don't speak, explain, negotiate, criticize, or argue with the child.
- Don't get intimidated if your child has a tantrum or refuses to go to time out.
- Use a timer to keep track of when time-out is over.
- Require the child to state what he did wrong and to apologize before he is allowed to leave time-out.
- Use a companion reinforcement program to positively reinforce appropriate behavior.

At this time, please complete the next worksheet to review the steps in using time-out and to get more practice in using the time-out tool to correct misbehavior. Keep in mind that it can take anywhere from a few days to a couple of weeks before your child will respond well to time-out. Try not to be discouraged and keep being consistent in applying time-out procedures. It might be a good idea not to go on to the next skill until you've had a few days practice with using time-out.

Using Time-out Worksheet

This worksheet is designed to give parents structured practice in using the time-out.

Step 1: Identify Target Behaviors

Complete the list below with specific target misbehaviors that you will consequate with time-out and the opposite appropriate behaviors that you will positively reinforce with a specific reinforcer.

Misbehaviors To Time-out
 A. Example: Interrupting parents during conversation.

1.   _____

2.   _____

Appropriate Behaviors To Reinforce

A. Example: Praise for not interrupting during parents' conversation.

1.   _____

2.   _____

Step 2: Choose A Time-out Place

The time-out place will be_____.

Step 3: Decide On The Length Of Time-out

Time-out will last _____ minutes for each of the above misbehaviors.

Step 4: Time-out Enforcement Checklist

- Get near the child and immediately instruct the child to stop the misbehavior.
- Warn the child that if he does not listen he will go to time-out.
- Wait five seconds and if the child does not comply send him to time-out.
- Don't explain, criticize, or lecture.
- Threaten the child with backup consequences such as removal of other privileges if the child refuses to stay in time-out.
- Use a timer to keep track of when time-out is over.
- After time-out is served have the child state what he did wrong and apologize.

Step 5 : Keep Track Of The Target Misbehavior

This step requires you to keep track of your progress.   For each of the target misbehaviors listed under Step 1, record the number of times per day the child exhibited each misbehavior. Remember, the child should receive a time-out every time he does not listen to your instruction first and then your warning to stop the misbehavior. By keeping track of the number of times each misbehavior occurs over a few days, you should be able to determine if time-out is being effective in decreasing the misbehavior.

Troubleshooting Problems with Time-Out

If the child…..	The parent should….
Talks to self in time-out	Ignore
Misbehaves in time-out	Ignore at first, if continues tell child to stop or use time-out back up consequences
Refuses to go to time-out	Take by hand and escort to time-out Carry young child to time-out For older children warn there will be backup consequences
Refuses to stay in time-out	Put in room with closed door. Open only if child stays in time-out. Lock door for short time (a minute or two) if child keeps coming out. Unlock and open door when child agrees to stay in time-out. Use back-up consequences
Refuses to leave time-out	Give clear instruction to leave time-out. If child does not comply extend the time-out

Skill # 5: Setting Up Standing Rules

Every parent should keep a list of a few standing rules that the child is expected to follow. Below are some examples of standing rules:

1. Homework is to be completed before dinner or you will not be able to watch television or play video games.
2. Bedtime is 8:30 pm Sunday-Thursday and 9:30 pm Friday and Saturday. If you stay up past your bedtime without permission, you will have to go to bed one-half hour earlier the next day.
3. Bookbags should be put in your bedroom when you come home from school. If your bookbag is left out, you will have to practice bringing it to your room five times.

After a standing rule has been established by the parent, it should be explained to the child.

Parents should post standing rules in one or two places in the home (e.g., kitchen, child's bedroom, playroom).

Parents should remind the child about the standing rule every now and then.

Standing Rules Worksheet

Write five standing rules that you will explain to your child. Include a consequence that will occur if a rule is broken. Post these standing rules in at least two places in the house.

1.

2.

3.

4.

5.

Skill 6: Managing Behavior Out of the Home

Noncompliant behavior often occurs in settings other than the home (e.g., while riding in the car, on shopping trips, in restaurants, while visiting in others' homes, in playgrounds).

It is often difficult to deal with noncompliant behavior in public places because you have less control over the environment, you may not want to draw attention from others, you may fear embarrassment if your child does not respond to correction appropriately, etc. Parents who effectively apply the parenting skills in their home will have a better chance of succeeding in public places. You shouldn't expect your child to behave in a public place if they don't behave well at home.

1. Have a plan. Plan ahead what action you will take if your child misbehaves outside the home. For example, if you are shopping and your child acts out, where will you send him to time-out? Will you find a spot in the store where he can stand alone for a few minutes? Will you return to the car and have him serve his time-out inside the car while you wait close by?

2. Explain your expectations to your child ahead of time and the consequences for his misbehavior.

3. Have a practice session. Tell your child what will happen if he misbehaves. Then practice it at home. For example, if shopping is a problem, make a short practice visit to a store where your goal is not to shop but to just practice positive behavior. If the child does well, get him a snack at the store as a reward.

4. During practice and in times of actual events, catch your child behaving well and provide praise.

5. Find ways to keep your child's attention focused in a positive way. For example: bring toys for the child to play with on a car ride; enlist the child's help in finding items in a supermarket; when visiting at another home excuse yourself regularly to praise your child for appropriate behavior.

6. Continue to give clear instructions when you issue a command. Get close to the child, make sure you have the child's attention, state your command simply and authoritatively, wait five seconds for compliance without saying anything else, and use time-out if the child does not comply.

Skill 7: Setting Up a Home Token System

A home token economy system can provide families with a positive method to promote behavior change. A token economy system is essentially a contract between the parents and the child stating that if the child behaves in a certain way, the parents will agree to provide tokens that can be traded for certain rewards and/or privileges.

As you read the steps in setting up a token economy, you will be required to write down exactly how you expect your child to behave, what you will do in response to such behavior, and the benefits or consequences that the child will receive for his behavior.

Acceptable behaviors are called "Start Behaviors" and unacceptable behaviors are called "Stop Behaviors." Start Behaviors are those behaviors that you expect your child to exhibit more frequently. Likewise, Stop Behaviors are those behaviors that you expect him to exhibit less frequently, or not at all. Writing down these expectations so everyone in the family understands exacly what is expected is a very important part of the token economy management program.

Use the Home Behavior Chart. The chart has space to record behavior for up to seven days. Each chart is divided into four sections:
1. Start Behaviors
2. Stop Behaviors
3. Rewards and Privileges
4. Total Tokens Remaining

To set up the behavior program, you must first complete each section of the Home Behavior Chart. A sample chart has been included to assist you as you construct the chart for your child. A blank chart can be found in the Appendix and it can be reproduced for your personal use. Use a separate Home Behavior Chart for each child in the family who will be involved in the program.

STEP 1: Start Behaviors
Begin by deciding on the behaviors you would like to list in the Start Behaviors section of the Home Behavior Chart. Refer to the sample list of start behaviors that follow to get an idea of what behaviors you may wish to list in the Start Behaviors section.

This sample list contains common behaviors that have been identified by other parents as desirable. Write down five or six behaviors (from the list or ones that you identified yourself) that you would like to see your child exibit more often.

Write these in the Start Behaviors section of the Home Behavior Chart. Be sure to include only those behaviors that you are certain your child is capable of doing if properly motivated. Avoid listing anything which is vague (e.g., "good attitude," "cooperative," "friendly," etc.). Only list observable and specific behaviors. For those start behaviors which can occur several times a day (e.g., "washes dirty dishes," "walks dog," or "puts garbage in garbage can," etc.), you should put the maximum number of times you will reward the behavior each day in brackets.

Next, assign a token value to each of the behaviors in the Start Behaviors section. The value should be between one and twenty-five tokens. To be effective, token values need to be high enough to encourage the child to display the behavior. Behaviors that are more difficult for the child, or which have more importance to you, should be assigned a higher token value. For instance, "practicing piano for a half hour" or "doing homework for one hour" should probably be worth more than "walking the dog" since these behaviors require more time and effort. It is important to immediately record the appropriate behavior on the chart after the behavior has occurred. In addition, parents should provide verbal praise to the child for good behavior.

Sample Start Behaviors

- awake and out of bed by   o'clock
- walks the dog (3x)
- makes bed
- leaves for school by   o'clock
- practices instrument
- puts dirty clothes in laundry
- mows yard
- starts/finishes homework on time
- studies for 60 minutes
- makes eye contact
- listens the first time asked
- throws out garbage
- uses manners at table
- reads for   minutes
- earns   grade in school
- makes plans with a friend
- washes car

- by   o'clock dresses self
- hangs up wet bathroom towel
- comes to dinner on time
- waters plants
- keeps room neat
- home by 10 p.m. weekdays
- completes chores list
- unloads dishwasher
- picks up laundry at dry cleaners
- in bed by   o'clock
- sets table
- speaks to others politely
- asks permission to borrow
- talks about feelings
- tells the truth
- takes medicine
- practices baseball 15 min. with younger brother

Extra Credit!

There is an additional line called Extra Credit in the Start Behaviors section. The child can earn extra tokens by displaying a behavior that is not listed as a start behavior, but which the parent would like to encourage and reward.

Home Behavior Chart

START BEHAVIORS	Value	Su	Mo	Tu	We	Th	Fr	Sa
1 Wakes up by 7 a.m	5		5	5	0	5	5	0
2 Walks dog after school	5	5	5	5	0	5	5	0
3 Puts schoolbooks in room	3		3	3	3	3	3	0
4 Cleans bedroom by dinnertime	5	5	5	0	5	5	5	5
5 Completes h.w. by 6:00 p.m.	10	10	10	10	10	10		
6 Writes phone messages (3x)	1	3	2	1	3	3	1	
7 Extra Credit! Reads 15 min. per night for 5 nights.	20	20						20
TOTAL TOKENS EARNED		43	30	24	21	31	19	25

STOP BEHAVIORS	Value	Su	Mo	Tu	We	Th	Fr	Sa
1 Interrupts others	5	5		5		5	5	0
2 Yelling in the house	5							0
3 Arguing with parents	10		10					0
4 Staying outside at dinnertime	35							35
5 No studying or homework	20					20		0
6								0
7 Extra Penalty								
TOTAL TOKENS LOST (Minus)		5	10	5		25	5	35

TOTAL TOKENS AVAILABLE		38	33	32	53	59	73	63

REWARDS/PRIVILEGES	Value	Su	Mo	Tu	We	Th	Fr	Sa
1 Extra 1/2 hour TV	25	25						
2 Buy a CD at store	35							
3 Free make bed pass	20		20					
4 Extra 1/2 hr on bedtime	25							
5 Tickets to ballgame	75							
6 Sleep over at friend's	35							35
7 Order a pizza	25							
8								
TOTAL TOKENS SPENT		25	20					35
TOTAL TOKENS REMAINING		13	13	32	53	59	73	28

STEP 2: Stop Behaviors

Refer to the list of sample stop behaviors below to get an idea of what behaviors to list in the Stop Behaviors section of the Home Behavior Chart.

This sample list contains common behaviors that have been identified by other parents as undesirable. Choose four to six behaviors from the list. Choose behaviors that you would like to see your child do less often or not at all. Write these behaviors in the Stop Behaviors section of the Home Behavior Chart. Be sure to include only those behaviors which you are certain your child is capable of stopping if properly motivated. Avoid listing vague behaviors. Only list observable and specific behaviors.

Then assign a token value to each of the behaviors in the Stop Behaviors section. The value should be between five and fifty tokens. A stop behavior that occurs frequently or has more importance to you should be assigned a higher fine value. The child should receive a fine or loss of tokens whenever he exhibits any of the behaviors in the Stop Behaviors section. To be effective, a fine needs to be strong enough to deter the child from displaying the behavior. Parents should immediately record the inappropriate behavior on the chart and should not engage in any verbal arguments or prolonged discussion with the child over the behavior.

There is an additional line called Extra Penalty in the Stop Behavior section. The child can lose tokens by displaying a behavior that is not specifically listed as a stop behavior, but which the parent finds extremely inappropriate and, therefore, worthy of penalizing the child by deducting tokens.

Sample Stop Behaviors

- sleeps past 11 a.m. on weekends
- fights with brother or sister
- whines
- comes home after 10 p.m. weekdays
- uses profane language
- talks back
- ignores parental request
- interrupts
- uses phone more than 2 hours per day
- not ready for school by   o'clock
- does not complete homework
- gets in trouble at school
- leaves bike, etc. outside
- tells parents to "shut up"
- teases younger sister
- messy room
- doesn't put dirty clothes in laundry
- slams doors
- cheats on test

- gives dirty looks
- borrows clothes without asking
- refuses to wake up in morning
- plays stereo too loud
- refuses to eat
- leaves without telling where
- smokes
- lies
- does not study for a test
- tattletales
- makes long distance calls
- gets poor grade in school
- has temper outburst
- refuses to take medicine
- argues with parents
- doesn't make bed
- sneaks food
- argues about a penalty

STEP 3: Rewards and Privileges

Select appropriate rewards and privileges that you think will motivate your child. Since kids differ widely in the activities they enjoy, it is important to involve your child in the selection of rewards and privileges.

Sample rewards and privileges are listed below. This list contains common rewards and privileges children find appealing. After reviewing this list with your child, decide which rewards and privileges should be included on the Home Behavior Chart. It is good practice to have at least six to eight rewards and privileges listed on the chart. Your child should have some latitude in deciding what rewards and privileges he would like. Many of the privileges on the chart will be activities that he may normally have been allowed to do, but will now have to earn (e.g., television time, staying up past a certain hour, use of the telephone).

As a general rule, the list should include rewards and privileges that the child could exchange for tokens fairly often, perhaps one or more times per day. Avoid listing many privileges that can only be used once a week or once a month.   For example, it might be better to offer a reward such as "1/2 hour of television time" (which can be given one or more times a day) than "money to spend when shopping on the weekend."

The final decision about a specific reward or privilege is left to you. You must consider the practicality of the rewards and privileges considering time, expense, and overall well-being of the child.

Next, assign a token value to each of the items in the Rewards and Privileges section. Determining the value of each item can be tricky. Costs should be low enough to give the child an opportunity to earn one or more rewards and privileges each day, yet high enough so that the child cannot earn privileges too easily. If he is earning a lot of tokens, it is usually a sign that the program is working well. Don't be reluctant to give frequent opportunities to exchange tokens for rewards and privileges.

Sample Rewards and Privileges

- sleep until   o'clock on weekends
- use of telephone for half-hour
- chooses restaurant for dinner
- permission for friend to sleep over
- trip to clothing store
- stays out until   o'clock
- allowed to visit a friend
- earns extra $
- able to use the car

- can buy a new CD
- ticket to see a movie
- permission to sleep at friend's house
- free chore day
- ride to school/from school
- extra half-hour video games
- extend curfew on Sat. night
- chooses activity with dad
- go fishing

STEP 4: Explain the Program to Your Child

Introduce the token economy system to your child in a positive manner. Explain that you have learned a method by which he might be able to earn rewards and privileges by behaving appropriately. Review the sample rewards and privileges list with the child and try to determine which items on the list are appealing. Add any other rewards and privileges you or your child can think of and then decide which ones should be written on the chart.

Review the behaviors you have selected for the Start Behaviors section Explain each one and briefly tell the teenager why you have considered putting this behavior on the list. Explain the behavior's reward value in tokens and discuss as necessary.

Review the behaviors you have marked down in the Stop Behaviors section. Explain each one and briefly tell the child why you have considered putting this behavior on the list. Explain the behavior's penalty value in tokens and discuss as necessary.

Once again, review the rewards and privileges that can be earned by accumulating tokens. With the child's input, modify this list (if necessary) to reflect your child's ideas as to what will motivate him to behave more positively. Explain the cost of each privilege and when privileges can be exchanged for tokens.

Go over the sample charts included in this chapter and explain how tokens are tabulated each day based on payoffs, penalties, and rewards and privileges used.

Set up a convenient time each day to review the child's performance for the day and tabulate the tokens earned, lost, and spent by the child. Put the total in the Total Tokens Remaining space.

Older children will understand the concept quickly. Some may object at first to the idea of having to earn tokens for privileges (some of which they may already receive automatically), but they usually agree to try out the program. Be positive when introducing the program to older children. Encourage cooperation. Avoid threatening or arguing about the merits of the program. Simply explain the features of the program in a firm, positive way but make yourself available for discussion.

Helpful Tips for Using a Token Program

- Verbally reinforce positive behavior as often as possible. Aside from the reinforcement the child earns by receiving rewards and privileges, praise and recognition are also powerful motivators for good behavior. Parents should take every opportunity to praise the child.

- Provide reinforcement immediately. Behavior that is reinforced immediately has the best chance of being repeated. Recognize and reinforce a start behavior right after it occurs, especially if it is a behavior which has been recently added to the chart.

- Avoid nagging and prompting. Parents should avoid nagging and should not repeatedly prompt the child to exhibit a specific start behavior. The child should not be given any tokens for start behaviors which occur after repeated prompting by the parent or other family member.

- Provide opportunities to spend tokens. Parents should think of success whenever their child is spending tokens and should, therefore, provide the opportunity for the child to cash in and earn rewards or privileges.

- Don't give second chances. Fine the child anytime he or she exhibits a stop behavior is on the chart. Giving a second or third chance to someone who is misbehaving only weakens the overall program.

- Don't engage in prolonged discussions or arguments. Children will often try to talk the parent out of giving them a fine for misbehavior and when this is unsuccessful, they may become argumentative. Avoid arguing. Record the fine on the chart with no further discussion.

- Don't allow hoarding. Some children prefer to save their tokens rather than spend them. Unless the child is cashing in tokens to earn certificates (which can be earmarked for a larger reward or privilege) tokens can lose motivating value if not exchanged regularly.

- Don't give loans. Parents may not loan tokens so that the child can receive a reward or privilege.

- Total tokens once a day. Set aside a time to total up the tokens earned, lost, or spent each day. Usually the best time to do this is in the late afternoon or early evening.

Skill 8: Using a Daily Report Card for School Behavior

A Daily Report Card can be used to improve behavior in school. It involves the collaboration between school and home in the assessment of the child's behavior by the teacher, and the administration of rewards and consequences at home, based upon the teacher's assessment. The program is similar to a token economy system described earlier. Parents of ADHD students are used to working with teachers. They quickly adapt to the Daily Report Card program and often appreciate having daily feedback as to their child's school performance. Daily reporting generally facilitates better parent-teacher communication and encourages the development of home-school partnerships. Parents don't have to wait for parent-teacher conferences or report cards to learn about their child's progress.

Use of daily report cards is quite common for children with ADHD. The immediate feedback provided by the teacher and opportunity to earn rewards at home and at school can be a great incentive for students. See the Apprendix for blank Daily Report Cards to use with your child..

Child's Name_____   Grade_____

Teacher_____   School_____

Week of _____   Days of the Week

	MON	TUE	WED	THU	FRI
1. Paid attention in class					
2. Completed work in class					
3. Completed homework					
4. Was well behaved					
5. Desk and notebook neat					
TOTALS					

Teacher's Initials   ____   ____   ____   ____   ____

N/A = not applicable   1 = Poor   4 = Good
0=losing, forgetting or   2 = Needs Improvement 5 = Excellent
   destroying the card   3 = Fair

Teacher's Comments
_____
_____
_____

Parent's Comments
_____
_____
_____

Child's Name_____   Grade_____

Teacher_____   School_____

Date _____   (Subjects/periods/teachers per day)

	____	____	____	____	____
1. Paid attention in class					
2. Completed work in class					
3. Completed homework					
4. Was well behaved					
5. Desk and notebook neat					
TOTALS					

Teacher's Initials   ____   ____   ____   ____   ____

N/A = not applicable   1 = Poor   4 = Good
0=losing, forgetting or   2 = Needs Improvement 5 = Excellent
   destroying the card   3 = Fair

Teacher's Comments
_____
_____
_____

Parent's Comments
_____
_____
_____

How To Use the Daily Report Card Program

The Daily Report Card shown is useful for children in grades one through eight. This card targets five behaviors commonly found to be problematic for ADHD children in the classroom. There are two forms of the program: a single rating card on which the child is evaluated once per day each day for the entire week and a multiple rating card on which the child is evaluated several times per day either by subject, activity, period, or teacher.

Most children in elementary school will be able to use a single rating cause they will be evaluated by one teacher one time per day. Those elementary school students who require more frequent daily ratings, due to high rates of inappropriate behavior, or because they are evaluated by more than one teacher each day, will need a multiple rating card scored by subjects or periods. Middle school students, who usually have several teachers in one day, will need to use the multiple rating card.

Regardless of whether the child is evaluated one or more times a day the target behaviors can remain the same and may include:
- Paid Attention
- Completed Work
- Completed Homework
- Was Well Behaved
- Desk and Notebook Neat

The student is rated on a five point scale (1=Poor, 2=Improved, 3=Fair, 4=Good, 5=Excellent). When a category of behavior does not apply for the student for that day, e.g. no homework assigned, the teacher marks N/A and the student is automatically awarded five points.

STEP 1: Explaining the Program to the Child
1. The child is instructed to give the Daily Report Card to his teacher(s) each day for scoring.
2. The teacher(s) scores the card, initials it, and returns it to the student to bring home to his parents for review.
3. Each evening the parents review the total points earned for the day. If the child is using the single rating Daily Report Card, it is to be brought to school each day for the rest of the week to be completed by the teacher. If a multiple rating Daily Report Card is used, then the child should be given a new card to bring to school for use the following day.
4. It is important that a combination of rewards and consequences be utilized since ADD children are noted to have a high reinforcement tolerance. That is, they seem to require larger reinforcers and stronger consequences than non-ADHD children.
5. Explain to the child that if he forgets, loses, or destroys the Daily Report Card he is given zero points for the day and appropriate consequences should follow.

STEP 2: Setting Up Rewards and Consequences

When using the Daily Report Card the parent should be careful to set reinforcement and punishment cut-off scores at a realistic level so that the child can be successful on the card provided that he is making a reasonable effort in school. Although individual differences need to be considered, we have found that a Daily Report Card score of seventeen points or more per day is an effective cut-off score for starting the program.

As the child improves in performance, the cut-off score can be raised a little at a time by the parent in accordance with the child's progress. If the child receives less than the cut-off number of points on any given day then a mild punishment (e.g. removal of a privilege, earlier bed time, etc) should be provided. For points at or above the amount expected, a reward should be forthcoming.

Constructing a List of Rewards

The child and parents should construct a list of rewards which the child would like to receive for bringing home a good Daily Report Card. Some sample rewards are:
- additional time for television after homework
- staying up later than usual
- time on video game
- a trip to the store for ice-cream, etc.
- playing a game with mom or dad
- going to a friend's house after school
- earning money to buy something or to add to savings
- exchanging points for tokens to save up for a larger reward

Constructing a List of Negative Consequences

The child and parents should construct a list of negative consequences one of which could be imposed upon the child for failure to earn a specified number of points on the Daily Report Card. Negative consequences should be applied judiciously given consideration for the ADHD student's inherent difficulties. Some examples are:
- early bedtime for not reaching a set number of points
- missing dessert
- reduction in length of play time or television time
- removal of video game for the day

STEP 3: Using the Program

During the first three days of the program, baseline data should be collected. This is the breaking-in phase wherein points earned by the student will count toward rewards, but not toward loss of privileges. As with any new procedure, it is likely that either the child or teacher will occasionally forget to have the Daily Report Card completed. Such mistakes should be overlooked during this breaking-in phase.

After this brief period it is essential that the teacher score the card daily. The teacher should ask the child for the card even when the child forgets to show it on his own. If the child repeatedly does not bring the card to the teacher for scoring the teacher should explain the importance of daily review of the card to the child. A mild consequence may be applied if the child continues to forget the card.

Generally the best time to score the card for elementary school students who are on a single rating system is at the end of the day. Middle school students, of course, should obtain scores after each subject. Ignore any arguing or negotiating on the part of the student regarding points earned. Simply encourage the child to try harder the next day.

Parents should be certain to review the Daily Report Card each day. It is not wise to review the card immediately upon seeing the child that afternoon or evening. Set some time aside before dinner to review the card thoroughly and dispense appropriate rewards or remove privileges if necessary. After reviewing the card parents should use a monthly calendar to record points earned each day for that month.

Other Great Parenting Programs

1-2-3 Magic

Dr. Thomas Phelan's *1-2-3 Magic* program began in 1984 and has been used by hundreds of thousands of parents, teachers, school administrators, and mental health professionals. His book by the same name has sold nearly one million copies, attesting to the popularity of this simple, yet powerful program that teaches effective discipline for children between the ages of two and twelve.

1-2-3 Magic is based on three steps for effective parenting. In step 1, parents learn to control their child's obnoxious behavior. Parents learn how to deal with whining, arguing, teasing, badgering, tantrums, yelling, and fighting. In this step parents learn to "count" obnoxious behavior. In step 2, parents learn how to encourage good behavior. Dr. Phelan reviews seven simple methods for encouraging positive actions in your child. Step 3 teaches ways parents can maintain healthy relationships with their child.

Dr. Phelan points out that there are two basic kinds of problems that children present to adults. Children are either (1) doing something you want them to stop doing or (2) they are not doing something you would like them to start doing.

Stop behaviors include such things as whining, disrespect, tantrums, arguing, teasing, fighting, pouting, and yelling. Start behaviors include positive activities like cleaning rooms, doing homework, practicing an instrument, getting up and ready in the morning, going to bed, and eating on time. Simple so far! A stop behavior is a behavior that your child is doing and you want them to stop. A start behavior is a behavior you want your child to begin. For stop behaviors Dr. Phelan recommends you use the 1-2-3 or "counting" procedure. For start behavior he recommends seven tactics: praise, simple requests, kitchen timers, the docking system, natural consequences, charting or the 1-2-3 variation. These will be discussed in a moment.

Stop behaviors require much less motivation than start behaviors. A stop behavior takes just a moment to complete while a start behavior may take anywhere from a moment to minutes or hours to complete. Picking up your shoes may take just a moment to do, homework may take an hour or more. The child has to begin the project, stay with it for some time, and then finish it. Putting an end to stop behaviors using the counting strategies in *1-2-3 Magic* is relatively simple. Encouraging start behavior is much harder.

Dr. Phelan recognizes that one of the biggest mistakes parents make in raising their children is that they think of them as little adults who are inherently reasonable and unselfish. Therefore, when one of these "little adults" is misbehaving, we make the mistake of assuming he probably just doesn't know what the right thing to do is and if he knew, he would stop misbehaving. Parents who make this assumption spend lots of time explaining why the child should behave better. For example, if Susie's brother, Jason, is mercilessly teasing his younger sister, Courtney, then parents operating under the "little adult" assumption would explain to Jason that teasing hurts Susie's feelings and that he wouldn't like it if someone teased him like that. These parents hope that by having such a conversation, their child will walk away enlightened and never tease Susie again. Parents know that this approach rarely, if ever, succeeds. Kids are just not well-intentioned, misinformed "little adults" who will stop misbehaving when they realize it is the right thing to do. Phelan points out that kids are not born reasonable and unselfish, they are born unreasonable and selfish.

To change that, Phelan advises parents to stop making two big mistakes: too much talking and too much emotion. Phelan noticed that too much talking can easily lead to too much emotion as parents get into what he calls the "Talk-Persuade-Argue-Yell-Hit Routine." Too much talking and explaining makes kids listen less and parents then become too emotional. All this emotion gives the child more attention and power and so they find your buttons and begin to push them. To stop this pattern, Phelan recommends that parents apply *1-2-3 Magic* and invoke the "No-Talking and No-Emotion Rule" when the child misbehaves.

Instead of talking and becoming emotional over a child's behavior, Phelan advises parents to respond to stop behaviors by counting, 1-2-3. You should count when your child argues, fights, whines, yells, throws a tantrum, etc. Do not use counting for start behaviors like getting up in the morning, going to bed at night, or getting your child to do homework. As Phelan says, the magic — or what seems like magic — is in the No-Talking and No-Emotion Rules, which make children think and take responsibility for their own behavior.

Phelan warns parents to do the 1-2-3 count properly. When you spot a behavior you want your child to stop you hold up one finger, look at your child, and say, "That's 1." If he continues to do what he is not supposed to you, let five seconds go by, then you hold up two fingers and say, "That's 2." If you get the same reaction you hold up three fingers and say, "That's 3. Take 5." You gave your child two chances to stop the behavior and if he didn't you gave him a consequence, a time-out period. The time out can be time (one minute for every year of age of the child) in a quiet place like a corner, on a stairway, in a room prepared for time-out, or to his bedroom.

If the child won't go to time-out after the parent gets to "3," Phelan advises parents to stay with the "No-Talking and No-Emotion Rule." Don't give in to the temptation to talk and threaten ("Come on now, do what I say. You won't have to stay in time-out for long. Do what I told you. Go to time-out now. Or else! Blah, blah, blah…"). Instead, you may have to escort the child to time-out (stay quiet, take him by the hand, carry him if you have to), but no hitting, spanking, or screaming. If your child is older (let's say eleven and up) and won't go to time-out peacefully, Phelan recommends you use a time-out alternative (earlier bedtime, reduction of allowance, elimination of television or video games). If your child continues to defy you and you are tempted to get into a screaming match, Phelan recommends you take a reverse time-out. Leave the room and go to your room, close your door, and calm down. But don't talk. And don't get stuck in the "Talk-Persuade-Argue-Yell-Hit Routine."

Dr. Phelan also addresses the worst nightmare of every parent, what to do when your child misbehaves in a public place. You know, places where you are most vulnerable to being embarrassed like Aunt Jane's house, a restaurant, the supermarket, etc. He advises parents to remain steadfast in applying the No Talk-No Emotion Rule and to count the child out. If you get to 3, find a time-out place (it could be a stairway in Aunt Jane's house, a place just outside the restaurant where you can watch the child, or a corner in the supermarket). If you can't think of a place you can always use the car for time-out.

In his book, Dr. Phelan gives tips to handle problems such as misbehavior in the car, sibling rivalry, managing temper tantrums, and pouting.

The second step of *1-2-3 Magic* focuses on encouraging good behavior. The emphasis here is on start behaviors. Remember, start behaviors are those behaviors you want your child to start doing: schoolwork, getting ready in the morning, going to bed on time, eating their dinner, cleaning their rooms, etc. It takes more motivation for children to start a behavior than it does to stop a behavior because they not only have to start the behavior, they have to finish it as well.

Phelan recommends that parents first work on stop behaviors using the counting strategy for one week to ten days before tackling start behaviors. He lists seven strategies for encouraging good behavior:
1.   positive reinforcement

2. simple requests
3. kitchen timers
4. the docking system
5. natural consequences
6. charting
7. counting (different version)

Positive reinforcement gives positive attention and praise to the child for starting and completing a task. It is important to use positive reinforcement often at the beginning of teaching a start behavior and keep it going as the child continues to demonstrate the behavior you want. Simple requests should be used to cue your child to start a behavior. When giving a simple request parents should make sure the tone of their voice is business-like and matter-of-fact and not emotional. Simple requests should be timed so that they have a better chance of being completed (i.e., don't call your child in to clean up his room when he is in the middle of playing with his friends…perhaps a better time would be when he is already at home). And requests should be in the form of a command not a question (i.e., "Clean your room now!" and not "Do you think you should clean your room now?").

Kitchen timers are good aids to encourage start behaviors. See if they can "beat the clock" when they do the task. Phelan encourages parents to use "the docking system" if a child does not start a behavior. For example, if the child is supposed to walk the dog after school and he does not, the parent may walk the dog for him, but charge the child a fee (part of the child's allowance) for doing it. Phelan also recommends the parent let the child experience the natural consequences of not doing certain behaviors. For example, the parent of a child who refuses to eat dinner might not get a second chance to have something to eat later. Charting behavior and providing positive reinforcement is another strategy that can improve start behavior. Charts can remind children to perform tasks and parents can use stickers as rewards. Lastly, parents can encourage good behavior by counting "1-2-3" if the child hesitates or refuses to start.

In his book, Dr. Phelan provides numerous examples of how to use these seven strategies to encourage good behavior. He discusses morning behavior, cleaning rooms, picking up, doing chores, behavior at mealtimes, homework, bedtime behavior, etc.

The last step in *1-2-3 Magic* is strengthening parent-child relationships. In this step Phelan focuses on ways parents can help build their child's self-esteem, the importance of giving praise and affection, the need to spend time one-on-one with your child, family time, and strategies to improve communication with your child by using active listening to encourage the child to express thoughts and feelings.

The principles in *1-2-3 Magic* have not been empirically and scientifically tested but it has passed "muster" by many parents who have found it easy to apply and successful. The best way to learn this program is to read Dr. Phelan's book or watch one of the video programs by the same name. By the way, he has adapted his program for use by educators so there is a *1-2-3 Magic* for teachers also. Additionally, if your have a teenager that is driving you crazy, try reading Phelan's book, *Surviving Your Adolescence*.

Collaborative Problem Solving

Dr. Ross Greene's book, *The Explosive Child*, contains the essential elements of a popular parenting program that Greene calls Collaborative Problem Solving (CPS). The basic premise of the CPS model is that the challenging behaviors of difficult, inflexible children should be understood and dealt with in the same manner as other learning disabilities. The assumption is that these children lack essential skills to manage frustration, maintain flexibility, and find rational solutions to problems. The goal of CPS is to teach these skills by helping parents and their challenging children work together.

As the name of his book implies, Greene focuses on children who are inflexible and explosive. He lists characteristics of inflexible-explosive children as follows:
1. Has difficulty managing and controlling the emotions associated with frustration and has difficulty "thinking through" ways to resolve situations rationally
2. Exhibits an extremely low frustration threshold and becomes frustrated far more easily and by far more seemingly trivial events than other children the same age
3. Exhibits an extremely low tolerance for frustration and is more easily frustrated and shows frustration more intensely than other children the same age
4. Has limited capacity for flexibility and is often unable to shift gears in response to commands or a change in plans
5. Tends to think in a concrete, rigid, black-and-white manner and does not recognize the gray in many situations

Greene states that many inflexible-explosive children have characteristics of ADHD and have associated deficits in executive functions, causing them to have difficulty regulating behavior and emotions and to plan their actions.

He describes a typical inflexible-explosive child named Casey, a six-year-old boy, who lived with his parents and younger sister. Casey was very hyperactive, had trouble falling asleep at night, could not play by himself, had difficulty transitioning from one activity to another, was limited in the clothes he was willing to wear and the food he was willing to eat, and was frequently irritable and easily agitated. He would have "meltdowns" several times a day.

Helen is another example of an inflexible-explosive child described by Dr. Greene. Seven years old, Helen was described as charming, sensitive, creative, energetic and sociable. Her parents also described her as intense, easily angered, quick to argue, resistant, and nasty when upset. She had a great deal of trouble making transitions from one activity to another and would "meltdown" when things didn't go exactly as she had anticipated. Greene tells the story of a day when Helen requested that the family have chili for dinner, her favorite food. Once her father prepared it for her she changed her mind and wanted macaroni and cheese. When her father told her he had already prepared the chili and could not make another dish, Helen got very upset. She could not let go of her desire for the macaroni and cheese and carried on with screaming and crying.

To help inflexible-explosive children, Greene encourages parents to create a "user-friendlier" environment at home. This is an environment in which the child's deficits in the areas of flexibility and frustration tolerance are less of a handicap. Parents in this environment will show the child that they understand how difficult it is for him to handle situations requiring flexibility and frustration tolerance. They will help the child maintain self-control when situations become difficult for him to handle. In such a user-friendly environment, Green advises parents to take the following steps.

1.   Be realistic about which frustrating situations your child can handle and be more open to eliminating unimportant, unnecessary frustrations.
2.   Think more clearly when your child is about to have a meltdown and take action to prevent it.
3.   Be attuned to situations that often cause frustration for your child.
4.   Move away from an adversarial relationship with your child, but at the same time maintain your role as an authority figure.
5.   Don't take your child's explosive episodes personally.

Greene cautions parents that when an inflexible child meets an inflexible parent, there is going to be a meltdown. One or both will become emotionally out of control. He advises that when a child is stuck in an inflexible mood, he will respond a lot better if he perceives adults as potential helpers, rather than as enemies.

To help you understand how to respond to events that affect you and your child, Greene asks you to picture three baskets in a row: Basket A, Basket B, and Basket C.

Basket A contains those important behaviors that are worth creating and enduring a meltdown over. For example, if your child is behaving in an unsafe way (i.e., running out into the street), you will need to put a stop to that regardless of whether the child has an emotional meltdown. Put behaviors in Basket A that you believe are very important to deal with and you are willing to go toe-to-toe with your child over if you have to. In a "user-friendlier" environment there are relatively few behaviors in Basket A.

Basket B contains those behaviors that are important, but aren't necessarily worth risking a meltdown over. This is the most important basket because it helps you teach your child the skills of flexibility and frustration tolerance. You use this opportunity to communicate with your child, help the child think through the situation, problem solve, and work it out. That is exactly what Greene recommends you do with Basket B behaviors—find ways to work it out with your child. Focus on problem solving. Help your child come up with ideas to solve the problem. To do this effectively, you will have to show empathy for the child's problem. Next, you will invite the child to solve the problem together with you.

Basket C contains unimportant behaviors that aren't worth even saying anything about. Basket C is usually very full. It contains lots of behaviors that you are willing to forget about altogether for the time being (i.e., not eating certain foods, not putting clothes away, looking away when told to do something trivial). You will accept the behaviors in Basket C and you won't even mention them as problematic anymore. You will let go of them completely.

Sorting Out Behaviors Worksheet

Take a look at the following common behaviors and decide what basket you want to put them in. Think about how you might respond to each behavior based on the basket you put it in. Check the basket. Suggest another adult in your family do this as well and see if you both agree on how important each behavior is and what your reactions should be.

		A	**B**	**C**
1.	crossing the street without looking	___	___	___
2.	leaving shoes in the living room	___	___	___
3.	dawdling in the morning instead of getting ready for school	___	___	___
4.	throwing a rock at younger brother	___	___	___
5.	refusing to get started on homework right after school	___	___	___
6.	talking back to mother	___	___	___
7.	calling sister a name	___	___	___
8.	arguing at the dinner table	___	___	___
9.	refusing to stay in time-out	___	___	___
10.	not starting homework at the scheduled time	___	___	___

The Practice Academy Approach to Changing Behavior

In their book, *Try and Make Me!*, Ray Levy and Bill O'Hanlon help parents understand the causes of defiant behavior in children and the steps that they can take to manage this behavior. You can get a lot out of reading their entire book as it is filled with many strategies found in traditional parent training programs. One strategy they present which is worth further discussion here is the use of the Practice Academy to stop inappropriate behavior and teach appropriate behavior.

Levy and O'Hanlon describe the behavior of Sammy Greene, a ten year old boy who looks like an angel when he is asleep, but becomes a package of trouble when he is awake. He gets up each morning with a defiant attitude and manages to turn what could be a simple task of getting ready for school into an all-out battle. He will fight with his mother over getting out of bed, what to wear, and when and what he wants to eat for breakfast. No amount of pleading, cajoling, or screaming by his mother could persuade Sammy to be more agreeable.

Levy and O'Hanlon point out that Sammy's defiant and moody behavior could be modified by putting him through an academy—a Practice Academy. As the name implies, a Practice Academy is a formal way of training your defiant child to replace his bad behavior with actions you approve. The program is based on the premise that when a defiant child refuses to do something, he is telling you that he needs practice in that skill. A Practice Academy provides such practice. It helps your child learn proper behavior by practicing it over and over and over and over again. Just like the way a math teacher might have students practice their multiplication tables until they do them perfectly.

There are four steps in a Practice Academy:
- First, you label the behavior and explain to your child that his behavior is telling you that he needs help changing the way he acts.
- Second, you pick a time to conduct a Practice Academy, if possible making it a convenient time for you and an inconvenient time for your child.
- Third, you have your child practice the behavior you want—over and over.
- Fourth, when the Practice Academy is over, you tell your child that he has done a nice job and casually announce that if similar problems arise again, it will be a sign that he needs more practice and you will be glad to give him another Practice Academy.

Suppose your child refuses to walk the dog, a responsibility he promised to take on when you agreed to have a dog in your home. When he refuses, you give your child a disappointed look and say, "Too bad. What your behavior is telling me is that you need a Dog Walking Practice Academy." Say that as calmly as possible giving him the impression that this is not a punishment, but an opportunity for him to practice the dog walking skill. You shouldn't be expressing any anger.

Next pick a time for the Practice Academy. Remember, it is important to pick a time that is convenient for you and inconvenient for your child. For example, you might pick a time when your child is just about to go outside and play with some friends.

At that time say, "Okay son. It's time to practice walking the dog. Let's do a Dog Walking Practice Academy." Instruct your child to sit on the living room couch. When you say, "Go and walk the dog," he should get the dog's leash, put it on the dog, and take him for a short (fifteen to thirty seconds) walk outside. Then he should come back in the house, take the leash off the dog, and sit on the couch. You should be close by, watching him each time.

If he does everything appropriately you can say, "All right. That was done well." Then, once again tell him, "Go and walk the dog." He has to complete the entire procedure again and again and again (perhaps five to seven times or more). Keep going past the point where you sense that it has become an ordeal for him. When the Practice Academy is over, remind him that you would be happy to give him another Practice Academy if he needs one. Avoid any sarcasm in your voice. This should be said in a matter-of-fact, non-threatening tone, helpful tone.

Let's turn back to Sammy, the youngster who would not get up in the morning and get ready for school in a pleasant way. When he is acting out in the morning, his mother would say, "Sammy, your behavior is telling me you need a Getting Up in the Morning and Getting Ready for School Practice Academy. When it is convenient for me I will give you one." Later, his mother might find a time when Sammy is planning to watch a favorite television show. She would say, "It's time to do a Getting Up in the Morning and Getting Ready for School Practice Academy." Sammy might reply, "No way. I'm watching television." Mom could respond by saying, "Not now. You will have to do your Practice Academy first. If not you will have to go to time-out until you decide to do it. Once you finish the Practice Academy, you can watch your television show. The sooner you get started, the sooner you will finish." Sammy stopped cold in his tracks and agreed to do the Practice Academy. He knew his mother meant business. She told him to sit on the couch and explained that to do the Getting Up in the Morning and Getting Ready for School Practice Academy, he would have to get into his pajamas, lie in bed, and when told to get up he should do so, get out of bed, get dressed, wash his hands and face, brush his teeth, and sit at the breakfast table. His mother had him repeat this over and over and over again. Watching him carefully to make sure he did each step.

Sammy's mother had to repeat the Getting Up in the Morning and Getting Ready for School Practice Academy with Sammy every night for the next four nights as he continued to display defiant behavior in the mornings. On the fifth morning, his attitude changed. He got out of bed, dressed, washed up, and came for breakfast without a complaint.

Summary

This chapter reviewed traditional parent training programs and other programs that teach parents how to manage difficult behavior. The traditional programs generally teach parents skills such as attending, rewarding, ignoring, instructing, the use of time-out, the use of home token programs, and daily report cards. Programs such as Russell Barkley's can be taught with groups of parents or individually. Other parent training programs such as those developed by Tom Phelan, Ross Greene, Ray Levy and Bill O'Hanlon offer other strategies that have been found to work well with children. While these other programs have not been subject to as much empirical research as the traditional parent training programs, they are very popular among parents. Hopefully, you will find the approach that works best for you and your child. I would encourage you to learn more about each of these programs by reading the authors' books.

Chapter 7   Strategies to Improve Learning in School

Children with ADHD have their greatest problems in school. It is pretty easy to understand why. Inattention, impulsivity, and hyperactivity combine to create a recipe for disaster for any child expected to listen, sit, and learn. Here's how these symptoms show up in the classroom.

Classroom symptoms of children with inattention problems:
- stares into space
- acts startled when his name is called
- has trouble working on his own and will need reminders to stay on task
- works at a slower tempo and will often run out of time before work is completed
- sluggish and will need prompts in getting started on work
- needs to have instructions repeated as the student may have been "tuned out" when the teacher provided instructions the first time
- looks confused
- makes careless mistakes in detail work such as math computation, spelling, grammar, etc.
- is disorganized. Misplaces materials and supplies necessary for work, can't find work
- has poor sense of time and often does not plan in advance so assignments are not finished on time
- has trouble starting assignments
- cannot stay focused when reading and often will avoid reading for this reason
- needs to reread material because forgets important points and details
- loses place when reading
- has trouble planning what to write for a writing assignment
- writes slowly and has trouble organizing his thoughts and putting them on paper

- loses interest in writing and becomes lax in following rules of spelling, punctuation, and grammar
- makes careless mistakes in math computation
- confuses one arithmetic operation for another because may not pay attention to signs
- forgets steps in solving multi-step problems

Classroom symptoms of children with hyperactivity-impulsivity:
- can't sit still
- talks excessively
- tips chair
- drops papers, pencils, and books on floor
- leaves seat without permission
- wanders around the classroom
- bothers other students
- trouble settling down, especially after a transition from an activity such as recess, lunch, or PE
- fidgets
- brings objects from home to play with at his desk
- calls out
- cannot wait his turn in games or in situations where taking turns is necessary
- wants things right away, cannot wait
- breaks rules often, even though he knows them
- accident prone
- drawn to exciting, risky situations
- starts tasks before the teacher finishes giving instructions
- starts tasks without reading written instructions carefully
- rushes through assignments and makes careless mistakes
- bothers others
- may act out when frustrated
- can show defiance and oppositional behavior
- over-reacts to frustrating situations
- poor self-control

When a student develops a problem in school, early detection and rapid intervention are desirable. Parents often find out too late when their son or daughter is having trouble. Sometimes parents and teachers may not notice a student who is struggling. Look for the early warning signs listed below:
- frequently complains about being bored in school
- has excessive absenteeism
- has a recent drop in grades
- lacks interest in homework
- has problems with tardiness

- talks about dropping out of school
- expresses resentment toward teachers
- rarely brings books or papers to or from school
- gets reports from teachers that the student is not completing work
- shows significant signs of disorganization (i.e., supplies not cared for)
- does work sloppily or incorrectly
- has an "I don't care" attitude about school
- has low self-esteem
- gets complaints from teachers that he/she is inattentive
- has trouble completing homework
- has school projects that are not complete or missing
- exhibits hyperactivity which interferes with learning
- fails to do assigned work in class
- hangs out with other students who are not doing well in school
- has trouble comprehending assignments when trying to do them
- has unauthorized absences from school

An Invisible Handicap

ADHD is an invisible handicap. Children with ADHD don't look any different than non-ADHD children. They generally don't have obvious speech, language, motor coordination, or mental handicaps that would make them stand out and give cause for concern. All children display some ADHD-like behavior. It is sometimes difficult to determine at what point normal inattention or restless, impulsive behavior becomes ADHD.

To complicate matters further, symptoms of ADHD are not consistently present within the same child in every situation. For example, the visual impairments of a visually handicapped child affect him in all situations. The same consistency is not always true for ADHD impairment. Because an ADHD student may be able to attend or be still in one situation and not in another, it is easy to suspect that the child may have more volitional control than he really has. "If he can do it now, why couldn't he do it before?" This leads us to expect more of the child than the child may be able to deliver. As Dr. Russell Barkley points out in his talks on ADHD, "The ADHD child succeeds once or twice and we hold it against him for the rest of his life."

Unfortunately, we don't have a very good answer to explain the inconsistency in the performance of children with ADHD. However, we do know that unlike other children, those with ADHD show an increased variability of performance. It is precisely this variability which is a hallmark characteristic of the disorder itself. Understanding teachers, rather than those who seek to discredit the disorder, look for confirming signs of the presence of the disorder in the student. They recognize the variability inherent in the behavior of students with ADHD and see inconsistency in performance as characteristic of the child's problems, rather than as evidence that the child "could really do it if he tried." They are less likely to describe the child as lazy or unmotivated and tend to see the child as having a problem rather than thinking of the child as being a problem. Teachers who have an understanding of ADHD are flexible enough in their teaching style to make accommodations for the child's handicaps and follow recommended educational interventions for the management of the disorder.

Critical Factors in Teaching Students with ADHD

Most children with ADHD can be taught successfully in regular classroom settings, provided teachers are willing to modify teaching practices to accommodate the child's special needs. Small changes in how a teacher approaches the child or in what the teacher expects can often be the difference between success or failure for the student. Some general principles for making accommodations for children with ADHD follow. You may want to share this information with your child's teacher(s).

Have Clearly Defined Rules
Children with ADHD function best in structured environments where expectations are clearly set by the teacher and consistent routines have been established. Classroom rules are an important part of this structure. To be effective, rules cannot just be posted and forgotten they should serve as a framework for guiding the student and teacher behavior throughout the year. Rules communicate the teacher's expectations regarding student behavior in the classroom. However, rules alone will not develop and maintain appropriate student behavior. They will be most effective when combined with teacher praise for desirable behavior and ignoring of undesirable behavior.
- Discuss appropriate classroom rules with the student.
- Write lists of rules on the chalkboard as students offer them.
- Choose four to six rules that are the most important and phrase them positively (e.g., Cooperate with others; Raise your hand to ask permission to talk; Complete work neatly and on time; Work at your desk quietly; Be prepared each day with your work).
- Print rules on posters and display them in the front of the room.

Develop Routines for Repetitive Activities
In every classroom, like in every home, there are routine activities that are performed daily. Children with ADHD perform better in highly structured classrooms with set procedures for carrying out activities.
- Develop structured routines to start the day in a consistent manner.
- Design a method of handing out and collecting papers.
- Designate a specific place the teacher keeps collected papers.
- Have students keep completed work in specific locations, e.g. notebooks, folders, etc).
- Use established procedures to check homework and classroom assignments.
- Establish routines for dismissal.

- Design procedures for dealing with transitions (e.g., short breaks, introduce new lessons with interesting joke or story, etc).
- Develop strategies for discipline and for administration of consequences.

Help the Student Stay Organized

As most teachers will readily attest, students with ADHD are generally not well organized. Their desks, lockers, book bags, or notebooks can be in shambles within days, if not hours, of just having been cleaned up and straightened out.   Parents of children with ADHD also have their hands full (often with the proverbial hair from their heads that they want to pull out), when they've spent all night with their ADHD child preparing homework, only to have it get misplaced or lost before it reaches the teacher. Teachers should place a high priority on being organized, even though the ADHD child may have a hard time doing so.

- Establish rules for neatness early on so that students appreciate your concern for quality work.
- Direct the ADHD student with organizational problems to straighten up his belongings and his work area daily. For elementary students, spot check their desks to encourage cleanliness and order.
- Check that notebooks have proper dividers for different subjects or activities and that the student uses clearly identified folders for work that is returned.
- Have the student write notes to himself for helpful reminders. Reinforce note writing strategies.
- Insist the student use a homework journal or assignment pad daily.
- Keep extra supplies on hand for the student to borrow.
- Have the student clear his desk of unnecessary material.
- Write assignments on chalkboard for the student to copy.
- Compliment the student when you note improvements in his neatness and organization.

Give Directions Carefully

Students with ADHD often are poor listeners. They distract easily and frequently miss important information said by the teacher. A common reason children with ADHD don't follow directions is they are often unaware that directions have been given.

- Before giving directions, get the full attention of the class. This can be done by changing the tone of your voice, flicking the lights on and off, closing the classroom door, or saying cue phrases like, "May I have your attention please?" to which the class has been conditioned to respond by listening for directions.
- Use short, simple sentences when speaking to the student. Be sure to give verbal instructions at the student's vocabulary level.
- Organize directions in sequence to avoid confusion.
- Give one instruction at a time. Avoid multiple commands.
- Give examples of what you expect the students to do.
- Check to be sure the student understands the directions. Repeat directions as many

times as necessary.
- Ask students to repeat the directions back.
- Write a summary of the directions on the chalkboard for easy reference or prepare assignments written on index cards.
- To reinforce a direction to an individual student, first make eye contact, then call the child by name and give the direction.

Find the Right Place To Seat the Student

Teachers rearrange seats once in awhile to find the right mix for students, especially those who are prone to be overly sociable or disruptive. Try to avoid sitting children with ADHD near each other, near windows, by bulletin boards, or close to areas of the room where they are subject to more distractions. The best seating is near a good peer role model and in close proximity to the teacher so that the child is easily accessible for teacher prompting, correction, or reinforcement.

Keep the Classroom Stimulating

The physical structure of a classroom can have a negative or positive effect on the performance of a child with ADHD. Early theories that children who are distractible will perform better in sterile, distraction free learning environments led special educators to seat children with ADHD in isolated study carrels, free of distracting stimuli or in classrooms with minimal room decorations, etc. Working on the "horse with blinders" theory to learning, these early educators were hopeful that with fewer distractions the ADHD child would be more able to attend to work and complete tasks. Unfortunately, many of these children were just as off task in this type of setting as in normal ones. What distractions the environment doesn't immediately provide to the child, the child will create for himself as desk chairs could easily become rockers, scraps of paper game pieces, etc. Much to the despair of his teacher, the child with ADHD manufactures distractions, perhaps in an effort to fight off boredom.

Teachers need to compete for the attention of their students with ADHD by creating as enriching and exciting a learning environment as possible, thereby increasing the child's motivation to attend. Sydney Zentall, Ph.D. (1990) stresses the importance of using colorful worksheets to stimulate the attention of students with ADHD and for teachers to incorporate into their instructional program creative learning experiences that fit the student's interests.
- Design your classroom with motivation in mind. Stimulating classroom decor with colorful and interesting surroundings has more of a chance at capturing the ADHD child's attention than blank walls.
- Classrooms that have centers of interest filled with ideas to stimulate creative minds and with enthusiastic teachers to keep those minds occupied work best for students with ADHD.
- Use an experiential approach to get the point of your lessons across. Find out what interests the student and go from there. Use his interests as a starting point and try to build on them.

Use Computers for Learning and Motivation

Teachers may find that computer assisted learning materials are better able to hold the interest of the ADHD student. Colorful graphics, interactive learning, and immediate feedback for responses act like magnets to attract attention. Teachers can use computer time as a reinforcement for good behavior at times during the school day.

Gear Assignments To Attention Span Not Just Ability

While children with ADHD sometimes have trouble getting started on assignments, they almost always have trouble finishing assignments. As one mother remarked:

"My child spent so much time in third grade in the nurse's office finishing his work, I don't know when he began anything new, because he had to keep finishing everything."

Closure is important to all of us and satisfaction comes from a job well done. How good could a child feel about himself if he is always "finishing" his work and trying to catch-up to others in class?

- Make allowances for the ADHD child's short attention span by shortening assignments.
- Give the child extra time to complete work if necessary.
- Provide breaks within a long work period.
- Use prompting, self-monitoring, contracting or other behavioral strategies to help the ADHD child stay on task.

Plan Ahead for Transitions

Students with ADHD often have trouble with transitions during the school day. Students probably make more than a dozen transitions each day. Transitions occur when:

- Students stay in their seats and change from one subject to another.
- Students change their seat to go to an activity in another part of the classroom.
- Students complete an activity and move back to their seat.
- Students leave the classroom and go to another part of the school.
- Students come back to their classroom after being in another part of the school.

Students and teachers spend a considerable part of their day in transition. Such times are often difficult for children with ADHD due to problems with disorganization and impulsivity. They have trouble settling down and getting their things together to proceed to a new activity. Particularly difficult for the ADHD student is the move from an unstructured activity (e.g., physical education, lunch, etc.) to a more structured one, that requires them to have self-restraint and work quietly. To assist students with transition, the teacher should:

- Establish rules for transitions. For example: Gather the materials you need, move quietly; Keep your hands and feet to yourselves; Get ready for the next activity.
- Review transition rules with the class until a routine is established.
- Supervise students closely during transition times.
- Provide immediate and consistent feedback to students who are doing well.

Help the Student Set Goals

Students with ADHD often have trouble setting goals and carrying out assignments, especially long-term projects. Book reports, science projects, term papers, etc. can present a challenge to the student and a headache to his parents. In order to set goals and finish assignments the student with ADHD will very likely need the teacher's help.

- Divide large projects into bite-size parts.
- Communication with parents to let them know what is expected and when things are due.
- Use homework journals and assignment time-lines for long term projects.
- Monitor the student's work carefully so he doesn't fall behind and get discouraged.
- Reinforce progress as work gets completed.

Provide Frequent Praise

By the time most students with ADHD have completed two or three grades in school, they have often had a stream of negative experiences with teachers. They usually have a hard time winning teacher approval and developing a positive relationship. As every teacher knows, the building of a positive teacher-student relationship is essential both to facilitate learning and to encourage the development of positive self-esteem in the student. Such a relationship, like any other meaningful interaction, must contain ingredients of caring, understanding, respect, and encouragement. In addition to bolstering shaky self-esteem, a teacher's positive regard will encourage students to put more effort into their work.

The first few days and weeks of school can be important as a tone-setter for the remainder of the school year. Many, although not all, children with ADHD are fairly well behaved in new situations and will generally show a honeymoon effect in school during the first few weeks. Teachers could take advantage of this positive display of behavior.

- Attend to the student's pro-learning behavior, recognizing efforts at achievement, and praising attempts as well as successes.
- Ignore minor negative behaviors and quickly attend to incompatible positive behaviors (ignore blurting out, praise hand-raising).
- Maintain close proximity to the child throughout the day by preferential seating close to the teacher or by the teacher walking near the student's desk.
- Spend one or two minutes each day to have a brief talk with the child.
- Keep a mental note of what kind of attention the child likes. When does his face brighten with pride? What words work to encourage? Does he respond to nonverbal reinforcers such as a smile, a wink, or a nod? Is he most proud when recognized publicly by verbal acknowledgments of his efforts or is he more motivated by the promise of tangible rewards?

Use Attention To Motivate

Teacher attention is an extremely powerful force in shaping behavior. Attention motivates students to perform, and the teacher is in a position to give positive attention to students contingent on their behavior. Most often, teachers will use attention to manage student behavior while students are involved in seated work activities. However, attention can be used to manage other activities such as those during instructional lessons, transition times, or unstructured class activities. In providing attention to students, teachers should consider the following procedures:

- Move about the room looking for opportunities to attend to positive behavior with praise.
- Scan the classroom frequently. Scanning lets children know the teacher is watching.
- Spot check the work of children who are good at looking busy but who may not be working.
- Praise the ADHD student frequently when you notice that he is complying with class rules.

Use Prudent Reprimands

Teacher reprimands for misbehavior are frequently used for classroom control. Prudent reprimands provide immediate negative feedback to the student. They should be delivered unemotionally, and briefly. When they are backed up with a mild punishment the reprimand may be even more effective at correcting misbehavior. Reprimands that are delayed, long-winded, and delivered in an emotionally charged style with empty threats of consequences are less likely to change behavior.

Give the Child with ADHD Responsibility

Giving the child with ADHD responsibilities that assist the teacher in managing the classroom can help the child feel like an important contributor to the class. Assig him leadership positions on team. Give him jobs at which he can be successful. Show the other students that you respect the ADHD student by trusting him to do a job. This can promote acceptance from others and build confidence.

Treat the Student with ADHD as a Whole Child, Not Just a Label

When students are diagnosed as having a disorder, there is a tendency to see them as they have been labeled rather than to view them as children. One can make arguments in either direction about the pros and cons of labeling children. Advocates for labeling would assert that labels drive services. Opponents point out that labeling of disabled children may make them even more "dis-labeled" in the eyes of those trying to help them. Clearly, we must appreciate the advantages and disadvantages of using labels to categorize students and we must always be cognizant that regardless of a common label, every ADHD child is different. Each has his or her own strengths and weaknesses and should be seen as uniquely individual.

What makes the student with ADHD exceptional is not his disability, but his ability. Teachers, through accommodating the student's needs by modifying the environment alone, will have only done part of the job. To do the rest we must see the child's strengths and help him build on them.

Summary

The core symptoms of ADHD, namely, inattention, hyperactivity, and impulsivity can manifest themselves in school in many different ways. Parents and teachers need to be alert to signs of this condition. After a diagnosis, teachers may be able to make their classrooms more "ADHD friendly" by incorporating relatively simple principles into their teaching style. There are several critical factors for teachers to remember. Teachers should become knowledgeable about ADHD and communicate frequently with parents and health care providers when they are called upon to do so.

Chapter 8   Handling Homework

"I have no life!" cried Ellen to her husband.
"Every afternoon all I do is homework. I can't take it any longer. It takes Sarah hours to complete work that should take just twenty minutes."

This is a common complaint of parents of children with learning disabilities and ADHD. Some children have trouble with homework because they just don't understand their assignments. Others understand the work, but they just can't pay attention long enough to get it done. Still others can't get motivated to sit down and do it. There are lots of reasons why kids have trouble completing homework. Parents have lost their hair (and their tempers) over homework. This chapter will offer some constructive advice to parents and some ideas for kids to help solve some of these homework nightmares.

Now, understand, homework isn't just a problem for kids with ADHD. It's just that when you have ADHD you are more likely to have homework problems. Problems with attention, memory, organization, planning, and sticking to a task are common in kids with ADHD—and homework requires a good amount of each of these. Most of the ideas and strategies found in this chapter will help children with ADHD, but they can be applied to any child with homework problems.

Why is Homework Important?

Homework has probably been around for as long as schools have been in existence. The purpose of homework is to reinforce and further the education of students. Many kids have trouble doing their homework or just don't seem to care about getting it done. Up to one-fourth of students in general education and more than half in special education have trouble with homework. Less than half of all high school students do all their homework. It is a source of stress for students, parents, and teachers alike.

Despite the problems with homework, teachers and parents realize the importance that homework plays in education. In their book, *Seven Steps to Homework Success,* Sydney Zentall and Sam Goldstein point out several constructive purposes for homework.

1. Homework will improve a student's achievement in general academic areas such as reading, writing, spelling, and mathematics, and in knowledge areas such as history and science.
2. Homework can improve a student's sense of responsibility and organizational skills, planning, and time management are learned through this process.
3. Homework can strengthen a parent's relationship with their child if things go smoothly.
4. For teachers, homework is a cost-effective way to deliver instruction.
5. Homework provides a method by which teachers can show parents what their child is learning in school.

So Homework is Important. Now, How Do You Get Your Child To Do It?

The answer is not simple. Children who have difficulty completing their homework will often need help. Not all parents have the time, interest, or the ability to provide such help. If you are willing to make the commitment to help your child get to the point where he can do homework independently, you will be making an important contribution to his future educational well-being.

Start by showing a strong interest in your child's learning. Talk about school every day. Encourage your child to share stories about his day in school. Find out what he likes best and what he is excelling in. Encourage him to express dislikes as well. Everyone needs to let off some steam and you can be a good sounding board for your child if he has a bad day at school.

Understand what your child's teacher expects. The type of homework your child brings home and other papers done in school will give you a pretty good sense of the work your child is doing. You should attend school-wide meetings such as annual open house meetings and others. Also make certain that you schedule private parent-teacher conferences a few times a year to get a more complete idea of what the teacher expects from your child and to check on your child's progress. Don't wait for an invitation from the teacher to meet if you think your child is having a problem. Make an appointment to talk. Don't show up unannounced.

Schools have homework policies and parents should be aware of them. Ask if homework is given every day and how much time your child should be spending on completing it. Find out if homework assignments are available on the Internet so you can keep abreast of your child's assignments. Inquire if your child's school has programs to help students who are having trouble with homework.

If your child has severe homework problems, then you, your child, and your child's teacher must form an alliance to provide the help that is needed. If a child is consistently being expected to do far more homework than he is capable of doing and this is resulting in very serious stress at home, it may be important for the parent and teacher to have a meeting to discuss this issue. Teachers are often parents themselves and will generally help parents find solutions to their child's homework problems. This may include reducing the amount of homework assigned to the child or encouraging the child to complete more work at school so there is less to bring home. The teacher could also help by making certain the child writes homework assignments in a planner each day, and can sign the planner and inform parents when assignments are not done at all or are incomplete. The teacher can also check that the child understands the assignment before leaving school.

Critical Skills Your Child Needs to Do Homework Independently

Zentall and Goldstein describe seven skills children need to be able to do homework independently. Parents and teachers need to encourage children to develop these skills and practice good homework habits when they are young. The sooner you start teaching these skills to your child, the better success he will have. To do homework successfully, the child must follow these steps.

1. Record the assignment and bring home the proper books and supplies.
2. Choose an appropriate place in which to complete homework.
3. Start assignments by reading directions and following them carefully.
4. Manage difficult or long-term assignments.
5. Maintain attention when assignments are boring.
6. Check work to make certain it is accurate and thorough.
7. Return homework to school and turn it in when it is due.

Record the assignment given by the teacher and bring home the proper books and supplies.
This seems simple enough. The child needs to write the assignment down when the teacher gives it. To make this easier, many schools give their students homework assignment planners. Some kids just don't use them. They have gotten into the habit of not writing down their assignments. They may not listen carefully when assignments are given, may not pay attention to details (e.g., page numbers, problems that have to be done, etc), and when they get home they don't have enough information to complete their homework correctly. Insist that your child use the planner every day to record homework. Ask your child's teacher to check to make certain your child has written the correct homework assignments in their planner. The teacher might agree to sign the planner each day so that you are certain the complete assignment was written.

Choose an appropriate time to start homework and a place in which to complete it. This can be a challenge. Children perform best with structure. It is up to the parent to set specific times for homework. Most homework battles are fought over when to start homework. Give your child some time to relax after school. Some kids need to have time to unwind, watch some television, and have a snack before settling down to homework. Get into an after school routine and make sure that homework time is a part of this routine. Every family's schedule is different, so I can't tell you what time homework should be done in your house. You can determine what the best time is for you and your family. Just make a schedule and work hard to stick to it. Remember, homework is non-negotiable. It must be done each day at the scheduled time.

Some children can only do homework when they are alone in a distraction-free area. Others can't stand to do it alone. They need to be where all of the action is—right in the middle of the kitchen where dinner is being prepared, the phone is ringing, neighbors are visiting, and brothers or sisters are talking. Within these locations, children have individual preferences. Some would rather work at a desk, others like to sprawl out on the floor, and for some, their bed makes the perfect place to do homework. Children, like adults, have different work styles. Parents need to help their child find the location that suits them best for doing homework.

Start assignments by reading directions and follow them carefully. Some children are not good at starting assignments and following directions. They don't know how to choose which homework assignment to start with. These kids need direction from others to get them to take the first step. Recommend that your child work first on the assignments that are easiest to do. This way they create some homework momentum. For tougher assignments, encourage your child to first try to solve problems on their own, but standby to offer help if needed. By the way, parents may not be the only homework helpers. Recruit siblings, friends, classmates, or relatives if you need them.

Manage difficult or long-term assignments. Children who are weak in this skill will probably need help in breaking projects into simpler tasks and scheduling when each task should be completed. Many kids are just overwhelmed by complex projects. They become nervous and can't decide on a plan. Their first reaction is to ask for help or to avoid the assignment. Review the assignment and try to explain it step-by-step. At first, your child may be too confused or too stressed to understand your explanation and you may need to take a break and come back to it. Use magic markers to underline important parts of the directions or important points in an assignment. Break large projects down into smaller tasks and set up a timeline indicating when a task is to be completed. Provide lots of praise when each task is finished.

Maintain attention when assignments are boring. Homework is boring for most children. For kids with ADHD, homework can be painfully boring. There are often plenty of things going on after school that are more fun to do than homework and these things often distract kids from focusing on their assignments. Provide some incentives for getting homework done. Motivate your child. Try using more frequent rewards. While it is not appropriate to bribe your child with expensive toys for doing homework, it is appropriate to offer the chance to earn snacks, extra screen time to watch television or play a video game, etc. You may also have to threaten

Seven Steps to Homework Success

Step 1   Write down the assignment given by the teacher and bring home the proper books and supplies.

Step 2   Choose a good time and place in which to complete your homework.

Step 3   Start each homework assignment by reading directions and following them carefully.

Step 4   Plan how to manage difficult or long-term assignments.

Step 5   Find ways to pay attention—especially when you get bored.

Step 6   Double-check your work to make certain it is accurate and complete.

Step 7   Return the homework to school and turn it in when it is due.

Note: from Sandi Sirotowitz, Leslie Davis and Harvey C. Parker (2004). Study Strategies for Early School Success. Florida: Specialty Press, Inc. Copyright 2004 by Leslie Davis and Sandi Sirotowitz. Reprinted with permission

loss of privileges to motivate your child to pay attention to homework. For example, have a standing rule that there will be no television or playing video games until homework is completed.

Checks work for accuracy and thoroughness. Many children rush through their homework and make careless errors. Children with ADHD often do not read directions carefully. It is important to help your child develop habits to check work. Encourage your child to scan completed homework pages for mistakes before putting the assignment away. Some parents like to check completed homework for accuracy. This is a good idea, but don't become too picky. Remember that homework is practice work intended to build an academic skill. Teachers generally do not expect perfect performance on homework and you shouldn't either.

Returns homework to school when it is due. This is a problem that drives parents nuts. You work all night with your child to get the homework done only to find that he left it in his room the next morning instead of bringing it to school. Or, he managed to bring it to school, but couldn't find it when it was time to turn it in to the teacher or didn't hear the teacher ask for it. Encourage your child to keep a separate homework folder. This is where completed homework should be kept before it is turned in to the teacher. If all the homework is in one place, it is less likely to be lost or forgotten. Parents may need to remind the child in the morning to review assignments due that day and check to make certain they are packed away for school.

Common Homework Problems and How to Solve Them

When Your Child Won't Do Homework Without You

If your child is becoming too dependent on you and won't do homework without you, it is time to think about ways you can help him do more on his own. One of the reasons your child may want help with his homework is that he may not have the self-confidence to try to do it alone. You can help him learn to be more confident by shaping his behavior. Here's how Eric's mother did so.

Eric is a fourth grader at Hawkes Bluff Elementary School in South Florida. He was one of those kids who did okay in school, but homework was a nightmare for him and his family. Eric insisted that he do his homework at the kitchen table within eyesight of his mother. Within a few minutes of getting started, he would ask for help. His mother would offer the help and when she would try to leave, Eric would panic and insist that she stay with him in case he had another problem. She would reassure him that he could do it on his own and would leave again, but the cycle continued and his mother would be repeatedly called back to provide assistance.

Eric's mother knew that he could do his homework on his own and decided to set limits on how much help she would provide. She told him that she would help him get started and then leave the room. He was not to call out for her and she would look in on him every few minutes. If he was working on his own when she checked on him, she would praise him. If he demanded help, she would tell him to do as much as he could by himself and she would leave. Within a week of doing this, Eric realized he did not need his mother's help as much as he thought. He developed the confidence to work on his own.

When Your Child Makes a Million Excuses to Avoid Homework

There are many children who have the ability to do their homework, but they lack the motivation. They procrastinate, find excuses to avoid doing homework, and seem to require repeated prompts from parents to get started. In this situation, a specific plan to solve the homework problem is necessary. Zentall and Goldstein suggest you follow these steps:

1. Encourage your child to take responsibility for homework, and don't allow yourself to get trapped in lengthy discussions or arguments. The message to your child should be clear: "Homework (or a percentage of it) must be completed."

2. Set up "homework rules" that you and your child can agree to follow. These rules provide structure and should include such things as when, where, and how homework should be done. Post these "homework rules" in your child's room and refer to them when a problem arises. Children will see them as rule-based decisions, rather than arbitrary commands.

3. Help your child make short-term homework goals that can gradually be extended. Some children become overwhelmed by the thought of too much homework. They need your help to break assignments down into "bite-sized chunks," which may be easier for them to manage. Each time a "chunk" is finished, offer some break time and encourage the child to tackle the next part of the assignment.

4. Reinforce and praise appropriate homework behavior and avoid getting into a negative pattern of scolding, nagging, or threatening your child. This will only increase frustration and tension, usually worsening the problem.

When Your Child Doesn't Understand Homework

Children should feel free to ask their parents for help with homework if they truly do not understand an assignment. Some kids may be embarrassed to ask for help and rarely do. Others skip difficult assignments entirely rather than seek help. Difficulty understanding homework is a common problem for children with learning disabilities, especially in the area of their specific disability (e.g., math, reading, written language). Parents who understand these learning problems tend to be very patient and supportive. Children with ADHD may also have learning problems of a different sort. They may become easily frustrated and impatient if they don't understand homework. Difficulties understanding and following directions are frequent problems for students with poor organizational skills and short attention spans. They don't pay attention to important information either in class or in written instructions.

1. Read directions over with your child. Underline important words in the directions. Break assignments down into simpler steps until your child understands what he is supposed to do.

2. Have the child read the directions to you, and ask that he explain them before beginning the assignment.

3. Stay with the child while he does a few of the problems. Provide praise for making a good effort and for following directions.

4. Talk with your child's teacher if he frequently has problems understanding his homework. Ask the teacher if it would be possible to make sure the child understands the homework assignment when it is given in class. Suggest that the teacher assign a homework buddy. At the end of the period or a day, your child and his homework buddy could meet to go over what needs to be done with homework.

When Your Child Gets a Late Start on Homework

Chronic procrastination with homework can become a bad habit. Parents should set limits and not allow the child to wait until the very end of the evening before getting to their homework.

1. Meet with your child and explain that putting off doing homework until the end of the evening is not a good habit. They are tired then and they won't have the proper energy to perform well. They may rush through homework and not do it correctly. If they need help you might be too tired to provide it at the end of the evening.

2. Set up a homework schedule that specifies when homework is to be done each day. This schedule may vary from day to day depending on the activities of the day.

3. Don't schedule too much into an afternoon and avoid evening activities that will cut into homework time. Make sure you are home to supervise and encourage good homework behavior.

4. Make a rule that homework must be completed before a certain time.

5. Withhold preferred activities until homework goals are accomplished.

6.. From time to time, arrange a fun evening activity (e.g., trip to get ice cream, playing a board game together, etc.) that your child can look forward to once homework is completed.

When Your Child Takes Too Long to Do Homework

Some children have a very hard time focusing when doing homework and they often go off task and waste a great deal of time. This is typical of children with ADHD who are either not taking medication or whose medication has worn off by the time they start their homework.

1. Meet with your child and explain that you want to work on a plan to help him complete homework in less time. Point out that this will give him more time to do things he enjoys.

2. Each day when the child gets started on homework encourage him to pay attention to his work for a specific period of time (maybe ten minutes at first) at the end of which you will check on him to see how he has done. Then, encourage him to work through a second time interval and so on. Gradually extend the work time to increase the child's length of independent work.

3. Instead of using time intervals as a goal, your child may prefer work goals. By breaking his work into smaller segments, he may feel less overwhelmed. If he tires, offer a break and perhaps a snack before he returns to work. Gradually extend the work goals to increase his length of independent work.

4. Avoid any pattern of repeatedly prompting your child to "get back to work" accompanied by nagging or scolding. Offer rewards and incentives for appropriate homework behavior.

5. Withhold preferred activities until homework goals are accomplished.

6. Many kids with ADHD waste a lot of time while doing homework. Thomas Powers, in his book *Homework Success for Children with ADHD,* recommends that parents set time limits for homework. The parent and child could determine how much time it should take to complete the homework assignments. The child is then only given that amount of time and, finished or not, when the time is up, homework is over. Many kids will realize that they need to dawdle less and work more efficiently to finish on time or they will not have their homework done for school the next day.

6. If your child is taking medication for his ADHD, schedule homework time when the medication has not worn off. Speak to your physician about the different kinds of ADHD medication available. Some are short-acting (last 3-4 hours), some are mid-acting (lasts 6-8 hours), and others are long-acting (lasts 10-14 hours). Your child may take a mid- or long-acting medication in the morning that has worn off by the time he starts homework. Your doctor may prescribe an afternoon dose of a short-acting medication to help him pay attention through homework time. Be aware, however, that taking stimulant medication in the evening may cause problems with sleep. See chapter 11 for more information about medications for ADHD.

When Your Child Doesn't Turning Homework In To the Teacher

Parents of children with ADHD often report that they discover their child's homework in their room when it should have been taken to school to be turned into the teacher. This comes after having spent hours on the homework the night before. Children who forget to bring homework from home to school should first try keeping a homework folder in their back pack. When homework is finished each night, children should get in the habit of putting it in the folder. Parents will need to remind the child in the morning to look over assignments due that day and check to make certain they are packed away for school in the proper folder.

Worksheets to Improve Homework Habits

Study Strategies for Early School Success by Sandi Sirotowitz, Leslie Davis, and Harvey Parker was written for children in grades three to six. It contains nearly one hundred work sheets that children can use to improve their study skills. I have reprinted some of the worksheets that have to do with homework and time management in this chapter. You may copy these and use them in your home. Please refer to the following pages.

- Homework Self-Check
  Have your child answer the questions and review with him his strong and weak homework skills. For skills that need strengthening refer to the earlier sections of this chapter for ideas.
- What is Your Time Schedule Like?
  Use this worksheet to begin a discussion of when and where your child prefers to do homework. Consider his suggestions before setting up the homework schedule in your house.
- Homework Planner
  Review this planner with your child if he has trouble writing homework assignments. You can make copies of this planner and require your child to use one each day.
- Direction Finder
  Use this worksheet to help your child identify words that give direction. When helping your child get started on homework, identify the "direction words" on the assignment.
- Solutions for Common Homework Problems
  Review this worksheet with your child. It offers solutions for common homework problems and gives the child the opportunity to think of others.
- Ask for Help When You Need It
  The child can identify people who can be sought out for help with homework when it is needed.
- Roadblocks to Concentration
  The child identifies things that disturb his concentration and finds solutions.

For additional worksheets to help children with homework refer to the following sources: *Study Strategies for Early School Success* by Sandi Sirotowitz, Leslie Davis, and Harvey Parker and *Study Strategies Made Easy* by the same authors.

Homework Self-Check

The seven steps to homework success are written below as a checklist. Read each step and check the category ("Always or Usually", "Sometimes", or "Hardly Ever") which best describes how you do your homework.

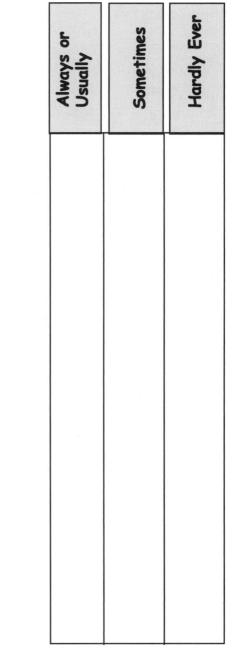

	Always or Usually	Sometimes	Hardly Ever

1. I write my homework assignments down every day and bring home everything I need to do my work.

2. When I can, I do my homework in the same place and at around the same time each day.

3. I start each homework assignment by first reading the directions carefully.

4. If I have a problem with an assignment, I know how to get help.

5. I know what to do to stay focused on my homework, and I take breaks when I need them.

6. I double-check my work to make sure it has been done correctly and completely.

7. Before leaving for school in the morning, I check to make sure I have my homework, and I turn it in to the teacher when it is due.

Which steps do you always or usually do?   ___ ___ ___ ___ ___ ___ ___

Which steps do you sometimes do?   ___ ___ ___ ___ ___ ___ ___

Which steps do you hardly ever do?   ___ ___ ___ ___ ___ ___ ___

What is Your Time Schedule Like?

Find a study place at home that works best for you, but first answer these questions.

HOW do I like to do my homework or study?
____ alone
____ with a friend or classmate
____ with my parents nearby

WHEN do I like to do my homework?
____ right after school
____ after I've had a snack
____ after I've had time to play or watch TV
____ after dinner
____ after my parents get home from work

WHERE do I like to do my homework or study?
____ in my room
____ in another room in my house where my family is
____ in a room near where my family hangs out
____ at a desk or table
____ on my bed
____ on the floor
____ wherever_____

Now that you know how, when and where to study, it is time to get down to work.

Note: from Sandi Sirotowitz, Leslie Davis and Harvey C. Parker (2004). Study Strategies for Early School Success. Florida: Specialty Press, Inc. Copyright 2004 by Leslie Davis and Sandi Sirotowitz. Reprinted with permission

Homework Planner

Name:			Day:		Date:	

Priority	Subjects	Homework Assignments	Due	Supplies Needed
	Language Arts			
	Math			
	Reading			
	Spelling			

Are all assignments copied? Yes   No   **Teacher's initials:**

Suggestions for using Today's Homework chart:
1. Write down all assignments and the dates they are due.
2. Check off each supply you need to take home.
3. Before leaving class at the end of the day put all the supplies you need in your book bag.
4. Decide the order of how you plan to do the assignments. Put the number in the "Priority" column.

Direction Finder

Read directions carefully before beginning work. When you read directions it is important to pay attention to the "direction words" that tell you how to mark your answers. In the directions below underline the "direction words" that tell you how to mark your answers.

Example: Draw a box around the right answer.

1. Circle the verb in each sentence.

2. Read each sentence and write the letter "N" if the underlined word is a noun.

3. Fill in the blank with the correct answer.

4. Copy the answer to each multiplication problem in the column to the right.

5. Find the mistake in each sentence and cross it out.

6. Shade in the circle next to the right answer.

7. Write a sentence for each spelling word on your list.

8. Select three of the five questions below and write your answers for each one.

9. On this quiz, you will need to match the word in the first column with its synonym in the second column.

10. Color all odd numbers blue. Circle all even numbers. If a number is odd and ends in the digit "3", draw a square around it.

Note: from Sandi Sirotowitz, Leslie Davis and Harvey C. Parker (2004). Study Strategies for Early School Success. Florida: Specialty Press, Inc. Copyright 2004 by Leslie Davis and Sandi Sirotowitz. Reprinted with permissio

Solutions for Common Homework Problems

Below are a few common homework problems and some solutions. Write another solution for each problem.

Problem: I am so busy with other activities after school that I don't have time for homework.

Solution 1: Skipping homework is not a choice. Choose one activity you won't mind skipping to make room for homework.

Solution 2: _____

_____

Problem: I get involved in watching television and before I realize it, I don't have enough time to do my homework.

Solution 1: A little television self-control is needed here! Tackle your home work first, then watch t.v. as a reward. If you are afraid you'll miss an important show—tape it! Once you get into the habit of getting down to work, it will be easier.

Solution 2: _____

_____

Problem: I forget to take my books home or I don't write down all of the assignments.

Solution 1: Use an assignment planner and check off the supplies you need for each subject. Before you leave school check your assignment planner again to make sure you have everything you need. Get in the habit of putting books you want to take home in your book bag right away so you won't be without them.

Solution 2: _____

_____

Problem: I can't get my homework done even though I spend a lot of time on it.

Solution 1: Be careful not to fall into some homework traps—start your work right away, skip problems that you don't understand then ask for help, be careful not to daydream (this wastes time), set a time limit for each subject and try to "beat the clock." Prom ise yourself a reward if you finish on time.

Solution 2: _____

_____

Note: from Sandi Sirotowitz, Leslie Davis and Harvey C. Parker (2004). Study Strategies for Early School Success. Florida: Specialty Press, Inc. Copyright 2004 by Leslie Davis and Sandi Sirotowitz. Reprinted with permission

Ask for Help When You Need It

"Why didn't you finish your math homework?" Mrs. Gordon asked Sam.
"I got stuck on problem seven and didn't know what to do." Sam replied.
"Next time ask for help!" advised his teacher.
Successful people know when to ask for help, and they are able to find others who can help them. Consider your family, friends, and others you know who you can go to for help. You may go to your mother for help in math, but your father for help in language arts. List the names in the spaces below.

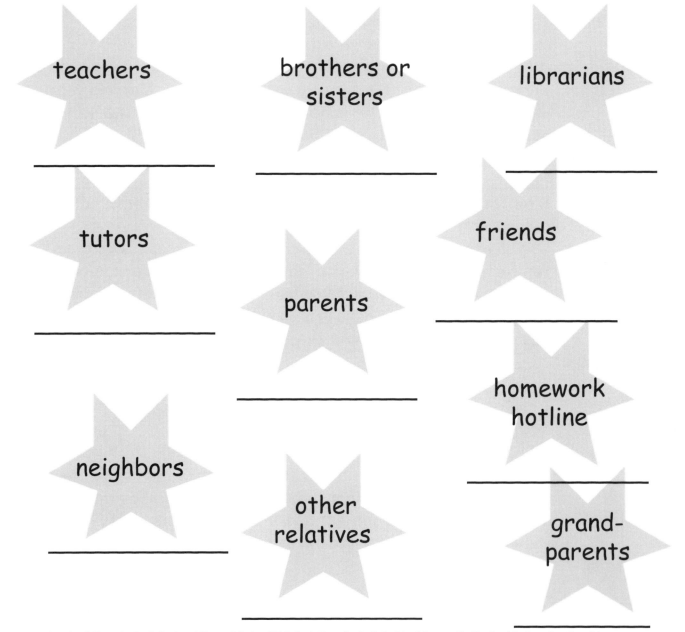

Note: from Sandi Sirotowitz, Leslie Davis and Harvey C. Parker (2004). Study Strategies for Early School Success. Florida: Specialty Press, Inc. Copyright 2004 by Leslie Davis and Sandi Sirotowitz. Reprinted with permission

Roadblocks to Concentration

There are a lot of things that can block us from concentrating. Below is a list of these "roadblocks to concentration". Circle the ones that make it hard for you to concentrate. Then, write down what you can do about it.

Roadblocks to Concentration	What I can do about it!
1. Music playing	_____
2. Computer games	_____
3. Other people	_____
4. Kids playing outside	_____
5. Pets	_____
6. Television	_____
7. Toys	_____
8. Telephone conversations	_____
9. People talking	_____
10. Brother or sister	_____
11. Tired	_____
12. Bored	_____
13. Hungry	_____
14. Restless	_____
15. Nervous	_____
16. Frustrated	_____
17. Confused	_____

Note: from Sandi Sirotowitz, Leslie Davis and Harvey C. Parker (2004). Study Strategies for Early School Success. Florida: Specialty Press, Inc. Copyright 2004 by Leslie Davis and Sandi Sirotowitz. Reprinted with permission

Chapter 9   Teaching Your Child Study Strategies

"True education is to learn *how* to think, not *what* to think."... J. Krishnamurti

This chapter reviews several study strategies that can help children understand *how* to learn more effectively in school. While parents may benefit from the information presented, you should encourage your son or daughter to look over the strategies presented in this chapter. For more detailed information about study strategies for children in grades three to six see *Study Strategies for Early School Success* and for secondary school students see *Study Strategies Made Easy* both by Leslie Davis, Sandi Sirotowitz, and Harvey C. Parker.

Organization

Students who organize their work, their time, and their belongings often do well in school. Disorganization is often cited by elementary and secondary school teachers as the biggest problem their students face. Students who are not well organized can easily lose track of what they are supposed to do and when. This strategy involves organization of school supplies, time management, and planning for assignments.

Organizing School Supplies

Let's start with the basics. The student should have adequate school supplies available for him to study properly and complete assignments. Below is a list of the minimum supplies a serious student should have on hand. Encourage your child to look over this list to determine whether anything is needed.

Get Ready! Get Set! Get Shopping!

Look over this checklist of school supplies. Put a check in the box next to the supplies you need. Then go shopping!

School Supplies Checklist

NOTEBOOKS, etc.
☐ one three-ring notebook or one per subject
☐ spiral notebooks, one per class
☐ dividers with pockets, a different color for each class
☐ case for highlighters, pens, pencils, etc.

ASSIGNMENT BOOKS, etc.
☐ student planning book
☐ calendar with enough empty spaces to write in
☐ electronic schedule and assignment keeper

IMPORTANT BOOKS, etc.
☐ dictionary
☐ thesaurus
☐ up-to-date atlas
☐ access to an encyclopedia
☐ library card

FILES, FOLDERS, AND BINDERS
☐ 3 X 5 or larger file box and ruled index cards
☐ an accordion file folder with enough pockets for each class
☐ crate to hold file folders for each class

OTHER NECESSARY STUFF
☐ pens, pencils, colored pencils, crayons, and erasers
☐ pencil sharpener
☐ ruler
☐ markers
☐ highlighters (yellow and at least one other color)
☐ glue, rubber cement, tape
☐ scissors
☐ stapler and staples
☐ hole punch
☐ paper clips
☐ rubber bands
☐ correction fluid
☐ reinforcers for notebook paper

Organize Your School Supplies

Did you buy your school supplies? Great! Now it is time to keep them neat and handy!

Start with your book bag (we like to "do the worst first.") Empty your book bag (but be careful to stand back so nothing that falls out bites you). Now be brave and look through what you've just dumped out.

<u>Yes</u> <u>No</u> Answer the questions by checking Yes or No:

____ ____ 1. Is anything moving or growling? Yes? Call the Humane Society. You can also reorganize what's inside:

____ ____   • are your pens and pencils in a case or box?

____ ____   • are your lunch snacks in their own plastic containers?

____ ____ 2. Are there papers you've been looking for and thought were lost forever? Yes? File them where you can find them easily, and follow ORGANIZE YOUR SCHOOL PAPERS YOU NEED NOW, found on page 112.

____ ____ 3. Are there papers you don't need to carry back and forth from school, but are taking up space in your bookbag? Yes? Separate them into piles and follow ORGANIZE YOUR OLD SCHOOL PAPERS YOU WILL NEED LATER, found on page 113.

Choose one day every week to reorganize your bookbag or to sort papers in your notebooks or folders. This can be boring, but it is very important to get into the habit of organizing your work at least once each week. Make this promise to yourself.

I will clean out my book bag every (circle one day):

Sun Mon Tues Wed Thurs Fri Sat

Organize Your School Papers You Need Now

You can use a 3-ring binder or folders to keep your papers organized. Read the suggestions below to help you organize the papers you need now.

3-Ring Binder

Use a 3-ring binder, with dividers, one per subject. Label each divider by subject name.

Folders with Pockets

Use pocket folders. Use a different color for each subject, and write the subject on the outside.

- Use a separate pocket folder with 3-hole clasps for homework (see the illustration below). Label the inside left pocket, "TO DO" for homework papers that need to be done. Use the inside right pocket to keep an assignment agenda page or homework calendar.

- Also buy a plastic sleeve with 3-holes to put into the folder. You will put your completed homework into the sleeve to keep it neat and clean and ready to turn in.

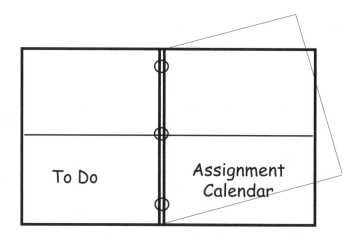

Homework Folder
2 Pockets-3 hole punched

Note: From Sandi Sirotowitz, Leslie Davis and Harvey C. Parker (2004). Study Strategies for Early School Success. Florida: Specialty Press, Inc. Copyright 2004 by Leslie Davis and Sandi Sirotowitz. Reprinted with permission.

Organize Your Old School Papers
You Will Need Later

There are some papers, like old tests, you will want to save to use later and some papers that you can throw away. Follow these six steps:

1. Separate your papers into two piles—TRASH and SAVE.
2. To Trash: doodlings, notes from friends, old homework papers, etc.
3. To Save: old tests with questions and answers written on them, class notes, important handouts.
4. Get manila file folders. Label them by subject and store them in a file drawer or plastic crate.
5. Write the subject, date, and page or chapter number on the top of each paper you file. When you are ready to study for a test, you will have an easy time reviewing old, but still important notes and tests.
6. It is important to get into the habit of filing your saved work every day.

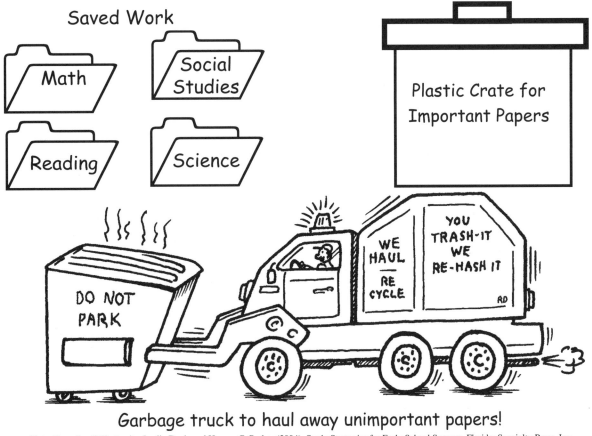

Garbage truck to haul away unimportant papers!

Note: From Sandi Sirotowitz, Leslie Davis and Harvey C. Parker (2004). Study Strategies for Early School Success. Florida: Specialty Press, Inc. Copyright 2004 by Leslie Davis and Sandi Sirotowitz. Reprinted with permission

Time Management

Use a "Do List" to help you organize assignments (jobs) that need to be done and to plan your time. Each day (or the night before), fill in the Do List with things that you need to complete the next day. Add items to the list each day such as specific homework assignments. Give each item on the list a priority number (1 is highest for the most important task) and do the assignments with the highest priority first. Color the star on the right when the assignment has been completed.

Do List!

Date: _____

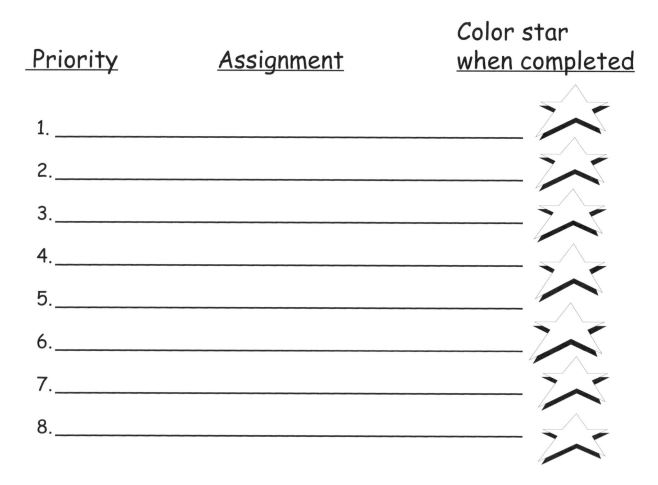

Priority	Assignment	Color star when completed
1.	_____	☆
2.	_____	☆
3.	_____	☆
4.	_____	☆
5.	_____	☆
6.	_____	☆
7.	_____	☆
8.	_____	☆

Note: From Sandi Sirotowitz, Leslie Davis and Harvey C. Parker (2004). Study Strategies for Early School Success. Florida: Specialty Press, Inc. Copyright 2004 by Leslie Davis and Sandi Sirotowitz. Reprinted with permission.

Weekly Planning

Use this weekly planner to schedule how you want to use your time this week. Block out times for after school activities, homework, and time to relax. Write the times of your favorite TV shows so you can plan to watch them.

Time	Monday	Tuesday	Wednesday	Thursday	Friday
2:00	_____	_____	_____	_____	_____
2:30	_____	_____	_____	_____	_____
3:00	_____	_____	_____	_____	_____
3:30	_____	_____	_____	_____	_____
4:00	_____	_____	_____	_____	_____
4:30	_____	_____	_____	_____	_____
5:00	_____	_____	_____	_____	_____
5:30	_____	_____	_____	_____	_____
6:00	_____	_____	_____	_____	_____
6:30	_____	_____	_____	_____	_____
7:00	_____	_____	_____	_____	_____
7:30	_____	_____	_____	_____	_____
8:00	_____	_____	_____	_____	_____
8:30	_____	_____	_____	_____	_____
9:00	_____	_____	_____	_____	_____
9:30	_____	_____	_____	_____	_____
10:00	_____	_____	_____	_____	_____

Monthly Planning

A monthly calendar with daily squares large enough to write notes on is an ideal way to keep track of activities, assignments, study times, tests, deadlines, and appointments that are planned throughout the month. Items should be transferred from the weekly planner to the monthly calendar and vice versa. This will provide an excellent way to scan a month's activities at a glance.

Other Time Management Tips

- Make good use of waiting time.
  It is estimated that people spend as much as an hour a day just waiting for something to happen. Use this time effectively. Carry a book, class notes, make calls, or catch up on homework while waiting.

- Traveling time can be time well spent.
  Most people spend a considerable amount of time each day traveling from one place to another. When driving or taking public transportation use the time for reading or review study notes to better prepare for future tests.

- Stay out of the habit of procrastinating.
  Try not to waste time by procrastinating. Get in the habit of starting things right away. Stop making excuses for getting things done. Recognize times you say phrases such as: "I'll do it later," "soon," "when I can fit it in," "not now," "tomorrow," "next week," and so on. Those who are truly committed to doing something either do it right away if time allows or schedule it in their daily, weekly, or monthly planner to be done later. Procrastination just keeps things "hanging over your head" and creates unnecessary stress. Challenge the reasons why you procrastinate. Fear, avoidance, laziness, and self-doubt are common reasons for procrastination. Once these issues are faced, there will no longer be a reason to procrastinate.

- Beat deadlines before they beat you.
  Be aware of deadlines. Set a deadline for tasks that need accomplishing and try to stick to it. Break complicated tasks down and set a deadline for completing each part.

Knowing Your Best Learning Style

Some students learn best by listening, others learn best by watching, and still others learn best by doing. These three learning styles are called auditory, visual, and kinesthetic. It is helpful for a student to know which style or combination of styles he prefers and use this when learning.

For example, if your child was given a list of words and their definitions to memorize, which approach would suit him or her best?

Visual Approach

- reads the words and definitions over and over.
- closes his eyes and "sees" them mentally.
- forms pictures of the words and their meanings.

Auditory Approach

- recites words and definitions to self.
- tapes words and definitions and listens to them repeatedly.
- listens as teacher or parents explain meanings.

Kinesthetic Approach

- writes the words and definitions.
- draws pictures to remember meanings.
- walks or moves around the room while concentrating on words and definitions.

It is also a good idea for students to be aware of the study environment in which they concentrate best. Most people become accustomed to studying in certain settings, at a specific time of day, and in a way that they feel most comfortable. Educators used to believe that ADHD students were more distractible than non-ADHD students and recommended they study in quiet, distraction-free environments. For some ADHD students this is true, for others it isn't. In fact, many people with ADHD say they concentrate better when there is background noise (i.e., music or television in the background). Some say they are more productive studying in the morning while others prefer evening. They may vary in the way they study as well (e.g., sitting up in bed and reading, sitting at a desk and writing notes).

Where, When, and How Do You
Do Your Best Work?

We all have different learning styles. Some people need absolute quiet around them when they read or study. Others are not bothered by noise. Music or the television playing in the background may even help them concentrate. Some kids like to do their homework in their bedroom, either at a desk or while lying in bed. Others prefer the kitchen or family room. What works best for you?

1. In which room of your house do you prefer to do homework?
   _____

2. Do you do homework in the same place almost every day?_____

3. When is the best time for you to study or do homework?
   a. morning   b. right after school   c. after dinner

4. Do you sit at a table or desk? _____ Do you prefer to lie in bed or sit on the floor when doing homework?_____

5. Do you like it quiet when you do homework or study?_____

6. Does it distract you to have music playing or the television turned on?_____ Do you like it when there is noise in the background as you do homework or study? _____

7. Do you usually know exactly what assignments you have to do?
   _____

8. If you get tired when studying, what do you do?
   _____

9. If you need help, what do you do?
   _____

10. Is there anything you could think of that would help you study better?
    _____

Note: From Sandi Sirotowitz, Leslie Davis and Harvey C. Parker (2004). Study Strategies for Early School Success. Florida: Specialty Press, Inc.
Copyright 2004 by Leslie Davis and Sandi Sirotowitz. Reprinted with permission.

Reading Comprehension Strategies

From elementary grades on, students must be able to read and understand and recall what information they read. This strategy emphasizes the importance of picking out the topic, main idea, and supporting details of a reading passage. By organizing this information, the reader will be able to answer questions of where, when, why, and how about the passage and write the topic, main idea, and supporting details down for notetaking. Picturing an umbrella is a good way for children to understand what they have read.

1. Picture an umbrella. The topic is the center of the top. You should be able to tell the topic in only one or two words.
2. The main idea covers the whole umbrella, just as it covers the whole paragraph.
3. The important details are the ribs that support the umbrella just as they support the main idea. Without support, both the umbrella and the main idea fall apart.
4. Finally, *get a handle* on the whole paragraph by paraphrasing what you have read.

Note: From Sandi Sirotowitz, Leslie Davis and Harvey C. Parker (2004). Study Strategies for Early School Success. Florida: Specialty Press, Inc. Copyright 2004 by Leslie Davis and Sandi Sirotowitz. Reprinted with permission.

Reading Comprhension Worksheet

Read the paragraph and use the umbrella to fill in the topic, main idea, supporting details and paraphrase below.

My sister is a bookworm. There are books all over the floor in her room and on her desk and chair. She also has three whole bookshelves filled with every book she has read. Any time you see her, she is reading. She reads in the car, on the bus and at home. Her backpack is full of books, and not just the ones she has to read for school. At night she reads under the covers with a flashlight. She even sleeps with books in her bed!

TOPIC OR TITLE

Main Idea

SUPPORTING DETAILS   SUPPORTING DETAILS   SUPPORTING DETAILS   SUPPORTING DETAILS

PARAPHRASE

Topic or Title: _____

Main idea: _____

Supporting details: _____

_____

Paraphrase: _____

_____

_____

Reading Comprehension Worksheet

Read the paragraph and use the umbrella to fill in the topic, main idea, supporting details and paraphrase below.

Central Park in New York City is a wonderful place to spend a spring day. On the weekends there are a lot of people skating, roller blading, and skateboarding. Many people sit on the grass and play guitars or flutes, or listen to musicians. People also visit the Central Park Zoo, which has many types of birds and other animals.

TOPIC OR TITLE

Main Idea

SUPPORTING DETAILS   SUPPORTING DETAILS   SUPPORTING DETAILS   SUPPORTING DETAILS

PARAPHRASE

Topic or Title: _____

Main idea: _____

Supporting details: _____

_____

Paraphrase: _____

_____

Summary

This chapter reviews several study strategies that can help children understand *how* to learn more effectively in school. Children with ADHD, due to inherent deficits in organization, planning, and attention, may benefit more than other children by learning study strategies. These study strategies can help them develop good habits with respect to organizing school supplies, managing time, dealing with projects, asking for help when it is needed, reading comprehension, and ways to improve their attention. This chaprer provided a very brief intro- duction to simple study strategies. For more information for children in grades three to six see *Study Strategies for Early School Success* and for secondary school students see *Study Strategies Made Easy,* both by Leslie Davis, Sandi Sirotowitz, and Harvey C. Parker.

Chapter 10   Understanding Your Child's Educational Rights

Parents as Advocates

Most parents of children with ADHD know that negative school reports are inevitable. As a parent, the last thing you want to hear is that your child is having problems in school. Although you've heard it before, its the type of news you never really get used to.

Parents can have different reactions upon hearing about their child's school problems. Some become defensive and angry. Their frustrations may spill over to the school and the teacher, quickly blaming them for their child's difficulties. Other parents avoid the problem, perhaps hoping it will subside on its own or the teacher will find a solution. Still, others become discouraged and essentially give up trying to solve their child's unending school problems. Most parents take a more productive stance. They meet with the teacher and others at school to develop a plan to help the child.

It is in the best interest of your child that you act as an advocate. If you don't stand up for your child and make sure your child is receiving an appropriate education, then who will? As an advocate you will need to know about the laws which were written to ensure that your child receives a free and appropriate education if he is attending a public school. You will also need to know how school systems function and what you, as a spokesperson for your child, can do to bring about changes that will benefit him.

Getting an appropriate education in our country is a right, not a favor. Laws such as the Individuals with Disabilities Education Improvement Act (IDEA 2004), Section 504 of the Rehabilitation Act of 1973, and the Americans with Disabilities Act (ADA) exist in the United States to protect people with disabling conditions from discrimination and to improve educational and other services available to them. These laws guarantee that your child has the right to a free appropriate education and that you, as a parent, have the right to participate in the educational process to make sure your child receives what he is entitled. If the educational process fails to work for your child, then it is up to you to make sure this guarantee sticks.

If you bought a stereo and it didn't work you could use the manufacturer's or seller's product guarantee to take action. You would return with proof of purchase, and either get it repaired or replaced or have your money refunded. You wouldn't wait for the company to call you to see how you liked their product. You wouldn't sit and complain and do nothing. You would take action. It's the same with the guarantee you have on your child's education.

If you think your child is not receiving an appropriate education you could use your guarantee (laws) to ensure that the school will find out if there is a problem and to provide the right solution (program or services) for your child. However, it is up to you to make sure that these laws are implemented properly. Your child's school will do some of the work for you, but in the end, it is up to the parent to monitor your child's progress. Parents can become great advocates for their child in school if they understand their legal rights and are willing to voice their concerns to the school when the educational process is not working for their child.

Many parents are reluctant to exercise their legal rights because they feel intimidated by their child's teachers and school administrators. Perhaps this is because, as children, most of us were taught to respect our teachers and to revere our principals. We were instructed not to question their authority, to always ask permission before speaking, and to follow their instructions to the letter or risk a poor grade, disapproval, or disciplinary action. Given such indoctrination, it is not surprising that, as adults, it is hard for many parents to overcome their apprehension when they come face-to-face with a teacher or principal and have to question the actions or opinions of the school. This is especially true if your child is having a problem in school.

If your child is a great student, having a parent-teacher conference is a piece of cake. The teacher lavishes one praise after another on your child, tells you that she wishes she had twenty-five more like him in the class, and compliments you on the superb job of parenting you must have done to create such a model citizen. You feel as if you got a straight A report card for being the world's most excellent parent and you leave the conference bursting with pride and eager to tell the whole world the great news.

If your child has ADHD, facing the teacher can be more like a nightmare than a dream. Chances are pretty good that you will leave the conference feeling depressed, demoralized, and defeated as a result of listening to a long litany of complaints about your son or daughter that you have heard many times before. You might feel as if you are to blame.

To be an effective advocate, it is important that parents take the steps listed below.

1. Learn about your child's disability and how it affects their education.
2. Understand the system of laws that exist to protect students with disabilities.
3. Become familiar with how schools function and the steps that are involved in accessing appropriate services.
4. Communicate effectively with school personnel.

Parents need to be empowered to advocate for their children in school. Empowerment enables people to obtain the knowledge, skills, and abilities necessary to make their own decision and gain control of their own lives. Empowerment is a natural process that often begins when you first learn that your child has a disability. Fearful that their child will not succeed in school, it is no wonder that many parents strive to gain some control over their child's schooling both to assist and to protect their child. If you are one of these parents, you are not alone. And if there is courage in numbers, then you should have plenty to spare, because there are hundreds of thousands of parents of children with ADHD who are feeling the same frustrations you are and who are learning to change, not just accept, the way schools currently educate their children.

Empowered Parents

- are motivated by the fact their child has a disability
- act on motivation by identifying resources and vowing to find others
- are proactive
- opt for the right path for the child even if it is more difficult
- make a powerful impact for themselves and others

Non-empowered Parents

- are not motivated
- accept things as they are and don't try to change things
- are reactive, not proactive
- choose the path of least resistance
- make very little difference in their family's life (much less in the lives of other families)

The Individuals with Disabilities Education Improvement Act (IDEA 2004)

The purpose of IDEA is to provide financial aid to states to ensure adequate and appropriate services for disabled children ages birth to twenty-one. IDEA has its roots in the Education for All Handicapped Children Act of 1975. IDEA has been amended several times, most recently in 2004.

To be eligible for special education under IDEA, the child must meet the criteria for eligibility contained in one of the eligibility categories in the law. These categories include: deafness, emotional disturbance, hearing impairment, mental retardation, multiple disabilities, orthopedic impairment, other health impairment, specific learning disability, speech or language impairment, traumatic brain injury, and visual impairment including blindness. If the child meets the criteria of one or more of these categories, requires special education or related services, and his disability adversely affects educational performance, the child may be eligible to receive special education and related services in school.

Students with ADHD may qualify for special education and related services under the category of "Other Health Impaired" (OHI). Eligibility criteria under this category requires that the child has a chronic or acute health problem that causes limited strength, vitality, or alertness with respect to the educational environment and results in an adverse effect on the child's educational performance to the degree that special education is needed. Some students with ADHD may qualify for services under the category of Specific Learning Disability (SLD) as many children with ADHD also have learning disabilities. Others with ADHD, who have serious emotional problems, may qualify for services under the category of Emotional Disturbance (ED).

A policy memorandum issued by the U.S. Department of Education in 1991 was sent to all public school agencies throughout the country. This memorandum clarified that ADHD was to be considered a disability under the OHI category and children with ADHD who were in need of special education and related services were eligible for such services on the basis of having ADHD alone. Nevertheless, many school districts did not have policies and procedures in place to adequately identify and place students with ADHD and therefore, many students with ADHD were not appropriately served by their school district. The final regulations of IDEA 1997 were published in 1999. ADHD was specifically named on the list of chronic health problems. This eliminated any ambiguity that school districts may have had about serving students with ADHD under IDEA.

Keep in mind that not all students with ADHD will qualify for special education and related services under IDEA. It must be determined that the disability significantly impairs the child's educational performance and results in a need for special education and related services. The impact on educational performance is not limited to academics alone, but can include impairments in other areas of school functioning such as impairments in socialization, emotional functioning, or behavior can be reason to need special education or related services as can deficits in study skills and work production that affects learning. Failing grades and low test scores are <u>not</u> a prerequisite for special education and related services.

Steps to Identifying and Serving Children in Need of Special Education and Related Services

Step 1. The child is identified as possibly needing special education and related services.

The "Child Find" program requires states to identify, locate, and evaluate all children with disabilities in the state who need special education and related services. To accomplish this, states conduct "Child Find" activities in which a child may be identified, and parents may be asked if the child can be evaluated. Parents who suspect that their child has a disability can also call the "Child Find" system and request an evaluation. A school professional may also ask that a child be evaluated to see if he has a disability. Parents may also contact the child's teacher or other school professional to ask that their child be evaluated. The request may be verbal or in writing. Evaluations need to be completed within a reasonable time after the parent gives consent.

Step 2. The evaluation.

A multidisciplinary team will be involved in the evaluation. The evaluation must assess the child in all areas related to the child's suspected disability. The results of the evaluation will be used to determine if the child is eligible for special education and related services and to make decisions about an appropriate educational program for the child based on the child's educational needs. If the parents disagree with the results of an evaluation, they have the right to take their child for an Independent Educational Evaluation (IEE). They can ask that the school system pay for this IEE. The team must consider the findings of any evaluation the student may have had by an outside source.

Step 3 Eligibility is decided.

The evaluation team and the parents look at the results of the child's evaluation. Together, they decide if the child is a "child with a disability," as defined by IDEA. If the parents disagree with the district's findings they may ask for a hearing to challenge the eligibility decision.

Step 4. Child is found eligible for services.

Once it is determined that a child is eligible for special education and related services, within thirty calendar days the Individual Education Program (IEP) team must meet to write an IEP for the child.

Step 5. An IEP meeting is scheduled.

The school district schedules and conducts the IEP meeting. The school staff must do the following: contact the participants including the parents; notify parents early enough to make sure they have the opportunity to attend; schedule the meeting at a time and place agreeable to parents and the school; tell the parents the purpose, time, and location of the meeting; tell the parents who will be attending; and tell the parents that they may invite people to the meeting who have knowledge or special expertise about the child.

Step 6. The IEP meeting is held and the IEP is written.

At the IEP meeting the team talks about the child's needs and writes the IEP. Parents and the child (when appropriate) are part of the meeting. If the child's placement is decided by a different group, the parents must be part of that group as well. The parents must give consent before the school system may provide special education and related services to the child for the first time. As soon after the meeting as possible, the child begins to receive services. Parents who do not agree with the IEP and placement may discuss their concerns with other members of the IEP team and try to work out an agreement. If they cannot resolve their differences, parents can ask for mediation, or the school may offer mediation. Parents may file a complaint with the state education agency and may request a hearing for due process, at which time mediation must be available.

Step 7. Services are provided.

The child's IEP must be implemented by the school as it was written. Parents are given a copy of the IEP and each of the child's teachers and service providers has access to the IEP and is aware of his or her responsibilities for implementing the IEP. This includes accommodations, modifications, and supports that must be provided to the child.

Step 8. Progress is measured and reported to parents.

The school must ensure that the child's progress toward the annual goals stated in the IEP is measured. The parents are regularly informed of the child's progress and whether that progress is enough for the child to achieve the goals by the end of the year. These progress reports must be given to parents at least as often as parents are informed of a non-disabled child's progress.

Step 9. IEP is reviewed.

The IEP team reviews the IEP at least once each year, or more often if the parents or school ask for a review. The IEP may be revised if necessary. Parents must be invited to attend these meetings and can make suggestions for changes within the IEP and can agree or disagree with the placement.

Step 10. Child is reevaluated.

Every three years, the child must be re-evaluated. The purpose of this evaluation is to find out if the child continues to be a "child with a disability," as defined by IDEA, and what the child's educational needs are. More frequent re-evaluations can be done if conditions warrant them or if the child's parents or teacher asks for a new evaluation.

What are the contents of the IEP?

The IEP must include certain information about the child and the educational program that is designed to meet the child's unique needs.

- *Current performance.* The classroom teacher, parents, service providers, and school staff provide information about the child's current educational performance.

- *Annual goals.* These are goals that the child can reasonably accomplish in one year. The goals are broken down into short-term objectives. Goals may be academic, social, behavioral, relate to physical needs, or address other educational needs. They must be measurable to enable others to evaluate if the student has achieved them.

- *Special education and related services.* There must be a list of the special education and related services to be provided to the child or on behalf of the child.

- *Participation with non-disabled children.* The IEP must explain the extent (if any) to which the child will not participate with non-disabled children in the regular class and other school activities.

- *Participation in state and district-wide tests.* The IEP must state what modifications in the administration of state and district-wide tests the child will need. In cases where a test is not appropriate for a child, the IEP must state why the test is not appropriate and how the child will be tested instead.

- *Dates and places.* The IEP must state when services will start, how often they will be provided, where they will be provided, and how long they will last.

- *Transition service needs.* When the child is fourteen years of age (or younger, if appropriate), the IEP must address the courses he needs to take to reach his post-school goals. There must be a statement of transition service needs in each of the child's subsequent IEPs.

- *Needed transition services.* Starting when the child is sixteen years of age (or younger, if appropriate), the IEP must state the transition services needed to help him prepare for leaving school.

- *Age of majority.* Starting at least one year before the child reaches the age of majority, the IEP must include a statement that the student has been told of any rights that will transfer to him or her at the age of majority.

- *Measuring progress.* The IEP must state how the child's progress will be measured and how parents will be informed of that progress.

Related Services

In order to benefit from special education, a child may require any of the following related services:
- Audiology services
- Counseling services
- Early identification and assessment of disabilities in children
- Medical services
- Occupational therapy
- Orientation and mobility services

- Parent counseling and training
- Physical therapy
- Psychological services
- Recreation
- Rehabilitation counseling services
- School health services
- Social work services in schools
- Speech-language pathology services
- Transportation

Section 504 of the Rehabilitation Act of 1973

In 1973, the Vocational Rehabilitation Act became law. As part of the act, Congress enacted Section 504, which provided that individuals cannot be discriminated against solely on the basis of their disability. Section 504 became the first federal civil rights law to protect the rights of persons with disabilities. Section 504 applies to all divisions of state government and all public or private agencies, institutions, and organizations that are the recipients of federal financial assistance. All local school systems in the United States are subject to Section 504 regulations if they receive federal aid through grant programs such as vocational education, Chapter 1, special education, and food/nutrition programs.

To be eligible for protection under Section 504 an individual with a disability means any person who (1) has a physical or mental impairment that substantially limits one or more of such person's major life activities, or (2) has a record of such an impairment, or (3) is regarded as having such an impairment.

If the school team determines that the child's ADHD does significantly limit his or her learning then the child would be eligible for a 504 Plan that would specify reasonable accommodations in the educational program and related aids and services, if deemed necessary (i.e., counseling, assistive technology). School personnel involved in general education, not special education, typically implement the 504 Plan. Students who receive services under 504 are not limited to only being able to receive accommodations and supports within the general education program. In fact, Section 504 does not limit the services provided or where the services may be provided, in regular or special education classrooms.

Sample Classroom Accommodations.
Below is a list of accommodations that may be put in a 504 Plan to accommodate students with ADHD.

Assignments/Worksheets
- extra time to complete tasks
- simplify directions

- hand worksheets one at a time
- shorten assignments
- allow use of word processor
- use self-monitor devices
- provide training in study skills
- break work into small parts
- allow use of tape recorder
- don't grade handwriting

Behaviors
- praise specific behaviors
- use self-monitoring devices or programs
- give extra privileges/rewards
- cue students to stay on task
- increase immediacy of rewards
- mark correct answers not incorrect ones
- use classroom behavior management program
- allow legitimate movement
- allow student time out of seat to run errands
- ignore minor, inappropriate behavior
- use time-out procedure for misbehavior
- seat student near good role model
- set up behavior contract
- ignore calling out without raising hand
- praise student when hand raised

Lesson Presentation
- pair students to check work
- write major points on chalkboard
- ask student to repeat instructions
- use computer assisted instruction
- break longer presentations into shorter ones
- provide written outline
- make frequent eye contact with student
- include a variety of activities during each lesson

Physical Arrangement of Room
- seat student near teacher
- seat student near positive role model
- avoid distracting stimuli (window, air conditioner noise, etc.)
- increase distance between desks
- stand near student when giving directions

Organization

- provide peer assistance with organizational skills
- assign volunteer homework buddy
- allow student to have an extra set of books at home
- send daily/weekly progress notes home for parents
- provide homework assignment book
- review rules of neatness on written assignments
- help student organize materials in desk/backpack,
- develop reward system for completion of classwork/homework
- teach time management principles
- help student organize long-term projects by setting shorter goals

Test Taking

- allow open book exams
- give exams orally if written language is difficult
- give take home tests
- use more objective tests as opposed to essays
- allow student to give test answers on tape recorder
- allow extra time for tests

Academic Skill

- if skill weaknesses are suspected refer for academic achievement assessment
- if reading is weak: provide previewing strategies; select text with less on a page; shorten amount of required reading
- if oral expression is weak: accept all oral responses; substitute display for oral report; encourage expression of new ideas; pick topics that are easy for student to talk about
- if written language is weak: accept non-written forms for reports; accept use of type-writer, word processor, tape recorder; do not assign large quantity of written work; give multiple choice tests rather than essay tests
- if math is weak: allow use of calculator; use graph paper to space numbers; provide additional math time; provide immediate correctness feedback and instruction via modeling of the correct computational procedure; teach steps to solve type of math problem; encourage use of "self-talk" to proceed through problem solving

Special Considerations

- alert bus driver to needs of student
- suggest parenting program
- monitor closely on field trips
- communicate with physician regarding effects of medication and other treatments the student may be receiving
- suggest other agency involvement as needed
- social skills training

- counseling
- establish procedure for dispensing medication
- consult with other outside professionals, i.e., counselor
- monitor medication side-effects

The Americans with Disabilities Act of 1990 (ADA)

The ADA guarantees disabled people access to employment, transportation, telecommunications, public accommodations, and public services. The ADA expands on the concepts and protections introduced by Section 504 of the Rehabilitation Act of 1973. It provides comprehensive federal civil rights protections for people with disabilities in the private and public sectors.

Section 504 or IDEA! How Should a Student with ADHD be Served?

Section 504 provides a quicker procedure for obtaining accommodations and services for children with disabilities than with IDEA. The eligibility criteria are broader, less information is usually required to determine eligibility, and less bureaucratic "red tape" exists to get services for the child. This may be quite satisfactory for children who have less serious disabilities. The more formal and rigorous procedures under IDEA, although time-consuming, offer better protections and safeguards for families than Section 504. Under IDEA, parent or guardian participation is required at each step of the evaluation, placement, or change of placement. These safeguards with respect to due process and discipline are particularly important when a change in placement of the child is being considered. The ADA provides an extra layer of protections for persons with disabilities in addition to those outlined in IDEA and Section 504.

For children whose disability is less serious, many school districts will encourage the use of Section 504 rather than IDEA. It is quicker, more flexible, and the district has greater latitude and less accountability for decision-making and enforcement. Since the early 1990's, school districts have focused heavily on procedures to better serve students under Section 504. Plans have been implemented to ensure that the student with ADHD will receive appropriate accommodations in the regular classroom. Commonly used interventions are: change seating, behavior modification, time-out, shortened assignments, one-to-one instruction, consultation with an educational specialist, peer tutoring, frequent breaks, and helping with organization. These and other accommodations and intervention strategies have been more fully discussed elsewhere in this book.

Many parents find that districts are reluctant to place children with ADHD in special education under IDEA within the Other Health Impaired category. Parents and guardians must evaluate their individual child's situation, the track record of the school and district in providing services under a 504 plan, and then determine the best option for their child.

Disciplining Students with Disabilities Under IDEA

Continued behavior problems is often a sign that the program that the child is receiving is not effective in addressing his educational needs. If parents believe that this is the case, they should write to the principal and request an IEP team meeting. At the meeting, the parents should discuss the problems the child has been having and the changes to the program that might help.

IDEA offers protections to students with behavior problems who are receiving special education services. The school must make sure that the student is not punished for conduct he or she cannot control; that such students get the services that are needed to learn to behave properly; and that the student is not unfairly disciplined. This becomes quite important for students with ADHD whose behavior can lead to disciplinary action.

A "Manifestations Determination Review" must be conducted before a student with a disability is suspended for more than ten days, expelled, or placed in another setting due to behavioral issues and violations of school rules. This review must take place within ten school days from the time the school decides to change the placement of the child because of a violation of a code of student conduct. The reviewers must consider each of these questions: Is the student's IEP correct? Is the student's school placement correct? Was the school following the IEP? Did the student's disability limit his or her understanding of the behavior in question or the consequences of such behavior? Did the student have trouble controlling the behavior due to his or her disability? If the reviewers decide that the student did not receive all required services, or that the child's disability affected his or her ability to understand or control the misbehavior, they must find that the misbehavior was a "manifestation" of the disability. If the reviewers decide that the misbehavior was <u>not</u> a manifestation of the disability, they can recommend that the student be subject to exclusion from school, including expulsion, on the same basis as students who are not disabled. The parents may challenge this decision through the special education procedural safeguard system.

If the conduct in question was caused by or had a direct relationship to the child's disability or the school's failure to implement the IEP, the student's conduct shall be determined to be a manifestation of the child's disability. Then the IEP team must conduct a functional behavioral assessment (FBA) and implement a behavioral intervention plan (BIP). It must also review and modify any existing BIP and return the child to the placement from which the child was removed. In addition, if the reviewers identify deficiencies in the child's IEP, the implementation of the IEP or the child's placement, there must be immediate steps taken to fix the problems. These same protections are available to students who are being considered for eligibility for special education even though they have not yet been determined to be eligible. Schools can remove a student with disabilities for up to forty-five school days without regard to whether the behavior is determined to be a manifestation of the child's disability in cases of: carrying or possessing a weapon; knowingly using, selling, or soliciting illegal drugs or controlled substances at school or school functions; or inflicting serious bodily injury on another person while at school, on school premises, or at a school function.

Differences Between IDEA, Section 504, and the ADA

IDEA	Section 504	ADA
Purpose		
To provide financial aid to the states in their efforts to ensure adequate and appropriate services for children with disabilities.	A civil rights law to protect the rights of individuals with disabilities in programs and activities that receive federal financial assistance from the U.S. Department of Education	A federal statute that requires businesses and other entities to provide reasonable accommodations to individuals who are protected by the Act.
Who is Protected?		
All children ages birth through 21 who are determined to be eligible within one or more of 13 categories and who need special education and related services.	All school-age children who meet the broader definition of qualified handicapped person; i.e., (1) has or (2) has had a physical or mental impairment which substantially limits a major life activity or (3) is regarded as handicapped by others. Major life activities include walking, seeing, hearing, speaking, breathing, learning, working, caring for oneself, and performing manual tasks.	Same broad definition as 504.
Responsibility to Provide a Free Appropriate Public Education		
Both IDEA and Section 504 require the provision of a free appropriate public education (FAPE) to eligible students covered under them. IDEA requires a written IEP document with specific content and required number of specific participants at the IEP meeting.	Section 504 does not require a document such as an IEP, but does require a plan. It is recommended that a group of persons knowledgeable about the student convene and specify the agreed upon services.	ADA does provide for FAPE to eligible students. The ADA has two provisions and services for eligible students with a disability. First, the ADHD applies its protections to cover nonsectarian private schools. Second, the ADA provides an additional layer of protection in combination with actions brought uner Section 504. and IDEA.
Funding		
IDEA provides additional federal funding for eligible students.	No additional funds are provided by Section 504.	No additional funds are provided by the ADA.
Regular vs Special Education		
A student is eligible for services under IDEA if it is determined that the student is disabled under one or more of the specific qualifying disabilities and requires special education and related services. The student must be provided services within the least restrictive environment. Special education and related services included within the IEP must be provided at no cost to parents. In addition, a full continuum of placement alternatives, including the regular classroom must be available for providing special education and related services required in the IEP.	A student is eligible as long as he or she meets the definition of a broadly defined qualified person. It is not required that the disability adversely affect education performance, or that the student need special education in order to be protected. The student's education must be provided in the regular classroom unless it is demonstrated that education in the regular environment with the use of aids and services cannot be achieved satisfactorily.	ADA does not address the provision of services within the regular or special education classroom. It broadens the policies set forth in Section 504. The public schools must provide appropriate accommodations. Related aids and services may be appropriate modifications.

IDEA	Section 504	ADA
Program Accessibility		
Requires appropriate modifications for eligible students.	Has detailed regulations regarding building and program accessibility.	Requires modification be made if necessary to provide access to FAPE.
Procedural Safeguards		
IDEA and 504 require notice to the parent or guardian with respect to identification, evaluation, and/or placement. Requires written notice with specifies required components of written notice. Requires written notice prior to any change of placement.	IDEA and 504 require notice ot the parent or guardian with respect to identification, evaluation and/or placement. Written notice is not required. Requires notification only before a "significant change" in placement.	Does not specify procedural safeguards for special education.
Evaluations		
A comprehensive evaluation which assesses all areas related to the suspected disability is required. The child must be evaluated by a multidisciplinary team or group. Informed consent required before an initial evaluation is conducted. Re-evaluation to be conducted at least every 3 years. Re-evaluation may be necessary before a significant change in placement. Provides for independent educational evaluation at district's expense if parents disagee with evaluation obtained by school and hearing officer agrees.	Evaluation must draw on information from a variety of sources in the area of concern. Decisions made by a group knowledgeable about the student, evaluation data, and placement options. No consent from parent or guardian required—only notice is required. Requires periodic re-evaluations. Re-evaluation is required before a significant change in placement. No provision for independent evaluations at district's expense.	Does not delineate specific evaluation requirements. However, appropriate modifications must be provided during an evaluation such as modifying entrance exams or providing readers or interpreters.
Procedures for Placement		
IDEA and 504 require districts when interpreting evaluation data and making decisions regarding placement to: • Draw upon information from a variety of sources. • Assure that all information is documented and considered. • Ensure that decisions regarding eligibility are made by persons who are knowledgeable about the child, the meaning of the evaluation data, and placement options. • Ensure that the student is educated with his/her non-disabled peers to the maximum extent appropriate (least restrictive environment).	IDEA and 504 require districts when interpreting evaluation data and making decisions regarding placement to: • Draw upon information from a variety of sources. • Assure that all information is documented and considered. • Ensure that decisions regarding eligibility are made by persons who are knowledgeable about the child, the meaning of the evaluation data, and placement options. • Ensure that the student is educated with his/her non-disabled peers to the maximum extent appropriate (least restrictive environment).	No specific placement procedures are required. However, appropriate modifications are required.

IDEA	Section 504	ADA

Enforcement

Enforced by the U.S. Department of Education, Office of Special Education Programs (OSEP). The districts response is monitored by the Staate Department of Education and OSEP. Potentially, federal funding could be withheld or a payback required should the district not be in compliance.	Enforced by the U.S. Department of Education, Office of Civil Rights. Potentially, all federal funding could be withheld should a state education agency or district not come into compliance.	Enforced by the Equal Employment Opportunity commission and the Department of Justice.

Grievance Procedures

Does not require a grievance procedure nor a compliance officer. Citizen complaints, however, may be filed with state department of education.	Districts with 15 employees required to (1) designate an employee to be responsible for assuring district is in compliance with Section 504 and (2) provides a grievance procedure for parents, students, and employees.	Does not require specific grievance procedures related to education.

Due Process

Parents have the right to participate in all IEP meetings and to receive notice of all procedural safeguards when the school district intends or refuses to take action or when a proposed change of placement or services is considered. Districts are required to provide impartial hearings for parents or guardians who disagree with the identification, evaluation, and/or placement, or any change of placement. The parent or guardian has the right to an independent hearing officer, present testimony and cross examine witnesses, and exclude evidence not presented by the opposing side at least five days prior to the hearing. The parent or guardian also has the right to be represented by counsel, and the right to a written decision within 10 days. IDEA has a "stay-put" provision. When the parent requests an impartial due process hearing, the child must remain in the current educational placement until all administrative and legal proceedings are finished. Suspensions or expulsions of a chid from school may trigger the "stay-put" placement provision if the parent requires a due process hearing to challenge the proposed suspension or expulsion. There is no similar "stay-put" provision in Section 504.	Section 504 requires notice to the parent or guardian with respect to identification, evaluation, and/or placement. Such notification does not have to be written. Notice is required before a "significant change" in placement is being made. Allows for the school district to appoint an impartial hearing officer. Requires that the parent or guardian have an opportunity to participate and be represented by counsel. Other details are left to the discretion of the local school district.	Does not delineate specific due process procedures. Individuals with disabilities have the same remedies which are available under Title VII of the Civil Rights Act of 1964, as amended by the Civil Rights Act of 1991.

Summary

Parents and teachers play important roles as advocates for children with disabilities. To be an effective advocate, they need to have an understanding of how the student's disability affects educational performance and what laws exist to protect disabled students. Federal laws such as IDEA, Section 504 of the Rehabilitation Act of 1973, and the Americans with Disabilities Act of 1990 ensure protections for children with disabilities. These laws differ in terms of how they each define who is eligible for such programs and services, how evaluations should be conducted to determine such eligibility, procedures for providing services, and safeguards for parents and guardians upon which to rely.

If a student is deemed eligible to receive services based on a disability, either a 504 Plan or an Individualized Education Program (IEP) will be written. These documents specify the services that will be provided to the student. Parents who disagree with any of the findings of the school can follow due process procedures to file grievances.

Chapter 11   Medication Management of ADHD

A multi-modal plan including medical management, behavior modification, educational planning, counseling, and parent education is usually recommended for successful treatment of the child with ADHD. This chapter will focus on medical management.

Medicine has been used to treat ADHD for nearly seven decades. The research on medical treatments for ADHD is abundant, and it clearly shows the efficacy of medications to treat symptoms of this disorder. The benefits have carefully been measured against the risks. The conclusion is that many children diagnosed with ADHD will be helped by medication. In most cases, medication will be the most effective treatment they will receive. This chapter will discuss the common types of medications used to treat ADHD, stimulants and non-stimulants, how they work to improve ADHD symptoms, the safety and efficacy of these medications, adverse effects, and recommendations for use of these medications. Information about commonly used medications to treat children with ADHD who have co-morbid disorders (anxiety, mood disorders, etc) will also be presented because co-morbidity is quite common in children with ADHD. This chapter is meant to serve only as an introduction to medication management. For more information the reader is referred to an excellent book by Dr. Timothy E. Wilens, *Straight Talk About Psychiatric Medications for Kids*. Please also note that while this chapter provides basic information about medications that are useful in treating ADHD, parents should consult their child's physician before making *any* decisions about the use of such medications.

American Academy of Pediatrics Guidelines for Treatment of ADHD

In 2001, the American Academy of Pediatrics (AAP) published clinical practice guidelines for the treatment of school-aged children with ADHD. The AAP recommended the following:

1. Primary care clinicians should establish a treatment program that recognizes ADHD as a chronic condition.
2. Appropriate target outcomes designed in collaboration with the clinician, parents, child and school personnel should guide management.
3. Stimulant medication and/or behavior therapy as appropriate should be used in the treatment.
4. If a child has not met the targeted outcomes, clinicians should evaluate the original diagnosis, use all appropriate treatments and consider co-existing conditions.
5. Periodic, systematic follow-up for the child should be done with monitoring directed to target outcomes and adverse effects. Information for monitoring should be gathered from parents, teachers and the child.

Physicians need the cooperation of parents and school personnel to ensure that the medication is needed, that main effects and side effects are monitored, and that it is available and is taken by the child as prescribed. Parents and school personnel should be responsible for giving medication to the child while in school. Some youngsters will forget to take scheduled doses of medication, others may be resistant to taking medication either because they don't like the way it tastes, they have trouble swallowing a pill, or they don't like the way they feel when they are taking medication. Teachers should be discreet when reminding a child to take medication in school. Taking medication is the child's private business and it should not be made public! Long-acting medications have greatly reduced the need for in-school dosing.

As the AAP recommends, medication should never be given without an established system to monitor its effectiveness. The doctor prescribing the medication should obtain information from parents and teachers. Typically, teachers are the best source of information about medication effects on the child with ADHD. Teachers may report information about the child's reactions to medication informally to the physician or they may complete similar forms as the parents for more systematic data collection. Use of behavior rating scales, such as the Conners Teacher Rating Scale-Revised (Conners, 1997) or similar ones, can be extremely helpful in determining changes in behavior. The ADHD Monitoring System, developed by Dr. David Rabiner, is a convenient program that parents can use to carefully monitor how their child is doing at school. By using this system, parents will be able to carefully track their child's progress in school and will be alerted as to when any adjustments or modifications to their child's treatment need to be discussed with their physician.

Parents and professionals can have access to the ADHD Monitoring System, the Vanderbilt Assessment Scales, and many other rating scales and history forms useful for assessment and monitoring by subscribing to a new website, myADHD.com (www.myadhd.com). Using this site, scales can be sent electronically by health care professionals, parents, educators, and others to easily obtain information about the child's progress. Parents and teachers can report information about medication reactions to the physician. This will give the physician an idea of how well the medication is working and if there are any adverse side effects.

If a child has been taking medication for ADHD for awhile, it is a good idea to have a no-medication trial in which behavior off medication could be observed by parents and teachers. For children on a stimulant medication, sometimes it is best to take the child off medication for a week about a month or so into the start of a new school year. This gives the teacher(s) a chance to have seen the child perform while on medication and compare the child's performance when no medication is given. For children taking a non-stimulant such as Strattera, it would not be advisable to stop the medication for a week because this medication needs time to build up in the bloodstream and medication-effects may take more time to diminish.

Stimulants

The stimulants are the drugs that are most commonly used to treat ADHD. This group of medications includes methylphenidate (Ritalin, Ritalin LA, Focalin, Concerta, Metadate, and Methylin) and amphetamine (Dexedrine, Adderall, and Adderall XR). The use of stimulants with children who have ADHD has been widely publicized and hotly debated. Are stimulants overprescribed? Do they cause long-term problems? Are they not just covering up the real, underlying psychological problems that children with ADHD have? Are physicians rushing to put children on medication without first doing an adequate assessment? Will stimulant use lead to substance abuse in the future? Why is the use of these medications so much higher in the United States than in other countries around the world?

Stimulant use has increased five-fold over the past dozen years and production of methylphenidate has tripled over a ten-year period. More than ninety percent of the methylphenidate produced in the United States is used domestically. The increase in use of stimulants has led to concerns about identification of ADHD in children, prescription for profit, and abuse of these medications. What explains this increase? Certainly more children are being diagnosed with ADHD than before. Prevalence estimates of the disorder were between three and five percent in the 1980's and now have reached as high as seven to twelve percent in children. However, ADHD may still be under-diagnosed and under-treated. One survey in four different communities found that only about twelve percent of diagnosed ADHD children received adequate stimulant treatment (Jensen et al., 1999). In contrast, another study in rural North Carolina found that many school-aged children on stimulants did not meet criteria for a diagnosis of ADHD (Angold et al, 2000). Also pushing the rise in methylphenidate use is the fact that stimulants are being dosed at higher levels and more frequently than before as clinicians realize the benefits of having kids on medication after school, on weekends, and during holidays. More diagnosis of adult ADHD has contributed to the rise in use as well since it is estimated that about one to three percent of adults suffer from ADHD and more are being treated than ever before.

The media has expressed concern about this dramatic increase in medication use. Fringe religious groups have prepared media campaigns designed to mislead, alarm, and provide biased information about stimulant medication. As a result, controversy continues to abound in the use of these medications for children with ADHD. The public is often confused by conflicting reports about safety and efficacy. However, there is no such controversy among the scientific community as to the safety and effectiveness of these medications.

How do Stimulants Work?

Stimulant medications increase activity or arousal in areas of the brain that are responsible for inhibiting behavior and maintaining effort or attention. They work by influencing the action of certain brain neurotransmitters, primarily dopamine and norepinephrine, both of which occur naturally throughout the brain, but are found in higher concentrations in the frontal region. The stimulants increase the amount of these chemicals that are available in the brain. Their action enhances executive functioning. These effects are observed in both ADHD and non-ADHD children, so the fact that a child improves when taking such medication should not be used to confirm a diagnosis of ADHD.

Stimulant medications are rapidly absorbed in the body, often within the first thirty minutes after taking them. Short-acting forms of stimulants (Ritalin, Methylin, Metadate, Focalin, Dextrostat, and Dexedrine) last three to four hours while mid- to long-acting stimulants (Ritalin LA, Concerta, Methylin ER, Metadate CD, and Adderall XR) last six to twelve hours. Thus, short-acting forms of the medication are often given two to three times per day. The longer-acting forms not only have the advantage of once-a-day dosing for many children, but they reduce the likelihood of multiple withdrawals from the medication per day due to wear off, the inconvenience and stigma of in-school dosing, the likelihood of greater compliance, and the lower abuse potential.

Parents often consider the school hours as the most important time when children should be on medication, but children with ADHD can benefit from taking medication that will last after school as well. Consider problems settling down and paying attention to homework, difficulties participating in sports after school, problems related to social behavior, noncompliance at home, difficulty waiting in restaurants or on long car rides, etc. All of these areas of functioning are important and stimulant medication may benefit the child in each of them. The final decision of whether to administer stimulants continuously during the day and throughout the evenings, on weekends, and holidays should be made by the parent in consultation with the child's physician as the risks versus benefits of medication are weighed.

There have been hundreds of studies on thousands of children with ADHD to support the fact that stimulants improve symptoms of ADHD. In general, seventy to ninety percent of children with ADHD will respond. That still leaves ten to thirty percent who may respond poorly or not at all, or who might have significant adverse side effects to the stimulants and cannot take them. A parent cannot assume that their child will benefit from stimulants. The only way to know is to try and see. Furthermore, while overall, methylphenidate and amphetamine compounds are similar, they do vary slightly in terms of specific action in the brain. Different stimulants may affect your child's ADHD symptoms to different degrees. If your child does not do well on Ritalin or Concerta, for example, he may respond very well to Dexedrine or Adderall XR. Parents should be patient and keep a scientific mind about them. Systematically try a medication at different doses and/or try different medications to achieve the optimal response. Parents will need to work closely with their child's physician to find the right medication and dosing and close communication with the child's teacher(s) will be necessary to measure the child's response.

For some children, medication will be enough to help them achieve in school and improve at home and socially. For others, a more comprehensive plan is needed that may include psychological and educational interventions. Researchers have conducted a number of studies to determine what types of treatment for ADHD are most effective, alone and in combination.

The MTA Study

The most comprehensive study to date (the MTA study done the late 1990's) investigated the effect of different treatments given to 579 children between seven and nine years of age who were diagnosed with ADHD, combined type. Children were divided into four treatment groups. One group was assigned to a medication-only treatment wherein they received carefully adjusted stimulant medication which was monitored every month by their doctor with the help of parents and teachers who rated the child's behavior and attention. A second group of children and their parents received a very comprehensive psychosocial treatment program to improve behavior, attention, social skills, and academic performance. Parents in this group attended thirty-five sessions of parent training to learn about ADHD and to acquire skills to manage child behavior. Children in this group were followed in school by a paraprofessional, received daily report cards to evaluate school behavior, and attended an intensive summer training program designed to teach social skills and self-control. A third group of children received a combination of carefully controlled medication and the comprehensive psychosocial treatments described above. A fourth group, the community control group, was sent into the community and instructed to get treatment for their child. Almost all of the children in this group received medication.

After fourteen months of treatment it was clear that the combination group that received both medication and psychosocial treatments improved the most in terms of core symptoms of ADHD as well as in overall performance. The group that performed second best was the one that received medication only. Medication seemed to have the strongest impact on the core symptoms of ADHD. Children who received psychosocial treatments alone did not do as well. Those who did the poorest were the children who were sent into the community to receive treatment. Even though most received medication, they were not as carefully monitored as the children in the medication only and combined groups.

The MTA study was the largest study ever done of ADHD treatments and has led experts to draw many conclusions about treatment. Below are three main points often cited.

1. Medication plus behavioral treatments work best for children with ADHD. Children with ADHD should receive multi-modal therapy.
2. Medication alone can be quite effective in reducing core symptoms of ADHD—inattention, impulsivity, and hyperactivity.
3. Medication was most effective when it was carefully adjusted to the needs of the child. Most children in the medication groups were monitored more frequently and treated with medication more vigorously than those in the community treatment group as they received higher daily doses generally given three times per day.

Documented Effects of Stimulants

To follow is a list of documented effects of stimulant medicines on children with ADHD.

*   reduced activity level to normal
*   decreased excessive talking and disruption in classroom
*   improved handwriting and neatness of written work
*   improved fine motor control
*   improved attention to tasks
*   reduced distractibility
*   improved short-term memory
*   decreased impulsivity
*   increased academic productivity (i.e., work produced)
*   increased accuracy of academic work
*   reduced off-task behavior in classroom
*   decreased anger, better self-control
*   improved participation in organized sports (i.e., baseball)
*   reduced bossy behavior with peers
*   reduced verbal and physical aggression with peers
*   improved peer social status
*   reduced non-compliant, defiant, and oppositional behavior
*   improved parent-child interactions
*   improved teacher-student interactions

Dosing of Stimulants

The dose of stimulant prescribed is not related to body weight but to how rapidly each child metabolizes the medication. A 180 pound adult may derive substantial benefit from 5 mg of Ritalin given three times a day, while a seventy-five pound child may need three times as much. Usually the child's physician will start with a low dose and gradually increase it until caregivers (parents and teachers) note optimal levels of improvement in behavior and attention. Refer to the charts in the following pages to see recommended dosing of stimulants and other medications for ADHD.

Emotional lability or hyperfocused (spacey) behavior seen within thirty minutes or a couple of hours after taking the medication may suggest that the dose is too high for that child. On the other hand, if the dose is not sufficient, the physician may increase it every five days or so until the child is functioning at the optimal level, if adverse side-effects become a concern, or if the maximum recommended dose is reached. With each adjustment in dose, the physician should obtain information from a caregiver (parent and teacher) as to how the child is functioning.

For short-acting stimulants, the average length of action is about four hours. However, for some children the medication may last only two or three hours, and for others, it may last five or six hours. Thus, the dose interval must be established for each child. Using feedback from parents and teachers (see www.myadhd.com) the physician may be able to determine when the medication is "wearing off" and when another dose should be given. Long-acting stimulants can take a child through the entire school-day but an additional short-acting tablet may be needed to get through homework and after school activities, hopefully, without significantly affecting appetite and sleep.

Long-Term Effects of Stimulants

The long-term effects of stimulants have not been carefully studied, but in the MTA study, the behavioral and cognitive effects of stimulants were monitored over a twenty-four month period. This is a relatively short term considering people with ADHD take stimulants for years. Nevertheless, findings from the MTA study showed significant reduction in the core symptoms of ADHD and associated problems of aggression and oppositional behavior as measured by teacher ratings and parent ratings.

There is no evidence that children build up a significant tolerance to stimulants even after taking them for years throughout childhood and adolescence.

Side Effects of Stimulants

Common side effects of the stimulants are: headaches, irritability, stomachaches, appetite loss, insomnia, and weight loss. About half of the children started on a stimulant will experience one or more of the common side effects noted above. Interestingly, this same percentage of ADHD children will complain about similar side effects when they take a placebo pill without any active medication. Stomachaches and headaches occur in about one third of children taking a stimulant.

Loss of Appetite. Decreased appetite occurs often and usually results in the child eating little for lunch due to the morning dose of medication. If a second or third dose is taken mid-day or later, this could affect appetite at dinner as well. For most children, however, their appetite returns after school, and they easily make up for the missed lunchtime meal. Parents should consult their doctor if appetite suppression is chronic and the weight loss is significant. Medication dose or timing may need to be modified. Give the stimulant medication with meals. Nutritional supplements can be added to the diet. Serving a hearty breakfast or late night snack may help and you can also offer your child high-calorie snacks, like ice cream.

Some of the infrequent side effects that can be caused by stimulant use include rebound effects,

DRUG	FORM	DOSING	SIDE EFFECTS	DURATION	PROS	PRECAUTIONS
METHYLPHENIDATE						
RITALIN METADATE Generic MPH METHYLIN	Short Acting Tablet 5 mg 10 mg 20 mg Chewable Tablet 2.5 mg, 5 mg, 10 mg Oral Solution 5mg/5ml & 10mg/5ml	Starting dose for children is 5 mg twice daily, 3-4 hours apart. Add third dose about 4 hours after second. Adjust timing based on duration of action. Increase by 5-10 mg increments. Daily dosage above 60 mg not recommended. Estimated dose range .3-.6 mg/kg/dose	Insomnia, decreased appetite, weight loss, headache, irritability, stomachache, and rebound agitation or exaggeration of pre-medication symptoms as it is wearing off.	About 3-4 hours. Most helpful when need rapid onset and short duration	Works quickly (within 30-60 minutes). Effective in over 70% of patients.	Use cautiously in patients with marked anxiety, motor tics or with family history of Tourette syndrome, or history of substance abuse. Don't use if glaucoma or on MAOI.
FOCALIN (with isolated dextroisomer)	Short Acting Tablet 2.5 mg 5 mg 10 mg	Start with half the dose recommended for normal short acting mehtylphenidate above. Dose may be adjusted in 2.5 to 5 mg increments to a maximum of 20 mg per day (10 mg twice daily). As above.	There is suggestion that Focalin (dextro-isomer) may be less prone to causing sleep or appetite disturbance.	About 3-4 hours. Most helpful when need rapid onset and short duration.	Only formulation with isolated dextro-isomer. Works quickly (within 30-60 minutes). Possibly better for use for evening needs when day's long acting dose is wearing off. As above. Expensive c	Similar to other short acting preparations.
RITALIN SR METHYLIN ER METADATE ER	Mid Acting Tablet 20mg Mid Acting Tablet 10 mg 20mg	Start with 20 mg daily. May combine with short acting for quicker onset and/or coverage after this wears off.	Insomnia, decreased appetite, weight loss, headache, irritability, stomachache.	Onset delayed for 60-90 minutes. Duration supposed to be 6-8 hours, but can be quite individual and unreliable.	Wears off more gradually than short acting so less risk of rebound. Lower abuse risk.	As above. Note: If crushed or cut, full dose may be released at once, giving twice the intended dose in first 4 hours, none in the second 4 hours.
RITALIN LA 50% immediate release beads and 50% delayed release beads METADATE CD 30% immediate release and 70% delayed release beads	Mid Acting Capsule 20 mg 30 mg 40 mg Mid Acting Capsule 10 mg 20 mg 30 mg	Starting dose is 10-20 mg once daily. May be adjusted weekly in 10 mg increments to maximum of 60 mg taken once daily. May add short acting dose in AM or 8 hours later in PM if needed.	Insomnia, decreased appetite, weight loss, headache, irritability, stomachache, and rebound potential.	Onset in 30-60 minutes. Duration about 8 hours.	May swallow whole or sprinkle ALL contents on a spoonful of applesauce. Starts quickly, avoids mid-day gap unless student metabolizes medicine very rapidly.	Same cautions as for immediate release. If beads are chewed, may release full dose at once, giving entire contents in first 4 hours.
CONCERTA 22% immediate release and 78% gradual release	Long Acting Tablet 18 mg 27 mg 36 mg 54 mg	Starting dose is 18 mg or 36 mg once daily. Option to increase to 72 mg daily.	Insomnia, decreased appetite, weight loss, headache, irritability, stomachache.	Onset in 30-60 minutes. Duration about 10-14 hours.	Works quickly (within 30-60 minutes). Given only once a day. Longest duration of MPH forms. Doesn't risk mid-day gap or rebound since medication is released gradually throughout the day. Wears off more gradually than short acting, so less rebound. Lower abuse risk.	Same cautions as for immediate release. Do not cut or crush.

This chart was updated 6/16/05. Consult with your physician before making any decision regarding medication usage.

DRUG	FORM	DOSING	SIDE EFFECTS	DURATION	PROS	PRECAUTIONS
DEXTROAMPHETAMINE						
DEXTROSTAT DEXEDRINE PDR does not list short acting Dexedrine tablets	Short Acting Tablet 5 mg 10 mg Short Acting Tablet 5 mg	For ages 3 -5 years: starting dose is 2.5 mg of tablet. Increase by 2.5 mg at weekly intervals, increasing first dose or adding/increasing a noon dose, until effective. For 6 years and over, start with 5 mg once or twice daily. May increase total daily dose by 5 mg per week until reach optimal level. Tablet is given on awakening. Over 6 years, one or two additional doses may be given at 4-6 hour intervals. Usually not need more than 40 mg/day.	Insomnia, decreased appetite, weight loss, headache, irritability, stomachache. Rebound agitation or exaggeration of pre-medication symptoms as it is wearing off.	Onset in 30-60 minutes. Duration about 4-5 hours.	Approved for children under 6. Good safety record. Somewhat longer action than short acting methylphenidate.	Use cautiously in patients with marked anxiety, motor tics or with family history of Tourette syndrome, or history of substance abuse. Don't use if glaucoma or on MAOI. High abuse potential particularly in tablet form.
DEXEDRINE SPANSULE dextroamphetamine sulfate ER	Long Acting Spansule 5 mg 10 mg 15 mg 5mg 10 mg 15 mg	In children 6 and older who can swallow whole capsule, morning dose of capsule equal to sum of morning and noon short acting. Increase total daily dose by 5 mg per week until reach optimal dose to maximum of 40 mg/day.	Same as above.	Onset in 30-60 minutes. Duration about 5-10 hours.	May avoid need for noon dose. Rapid onset. Good safety record.	As above. Less likely to be abused intranasal or IV than short acting. Must use whole capsule.
MIXED AMPHETAMINE						
ADDERALL	Short Acting Tablet 5 mg 7.5 mg 10 mg 12.5 mg 15 mg 20 mg 30 mg	Starting dose is 5 or 10 mg each morning (age 6 and older). May be adjusted in 5-10 mg increments up to 30 mg per day.	Same as above.	Onset in 30-60 minutes. Duration about 4-5 hours.	Wears off more gradually than dextroamphetamine alone, so rebound is less likely and more mild.	Same as for Dexedrine tablets.
ADDERALL XR 50% immediate release beads and 50% delayed release beads	Long Acting Capsule 5 mg 10 mg 15 mg 20 mg 25 mg 30 mg	Starting dose is 5 or 10 mg each morning (age 6 and older). May be adjusted in 5-10 mg increments up to 30 mg per day.	Same as above.	Onset in 60-90 minutes (possibly sooner). Duration 10-12 hours.	May swallow whole or sprinkle ALL contents on a spoonful of applesauce. May last longer than most other sustained release stimulants. Less likely rebound than with long acting dextroamphetamine.	Same as for Dexedrine Spansules except that it has documented efficacy when sprinkled on applesauce.
ATOMOXETINE						
STRATTERA	Long Acting Capsule 10 mg 18 mg 25 mg 40 mg 60 mg	Starting dose is 0.5 mg/kg. The targeted clinical dose is approximately 1.2 mg/kg. Increase at weekly intervals. Medication must be used each day. Usually started in the morning, but may be changed to evening. It may be divided into a morning and an evening dose, particularly if need higher doses.	In children: decreased appetite, GI upset (can be reduced if medication taken with food), sedation (can be reduced by dosing in evening), lightheadedness. In adults: insomnia, sexual side effects, increased blood pressure.	Starts working within a few days to one week, but full effect may not be evident for a month or more. Duration all day (24/7) so long as taken daily as directed.	Avoids problems of rebound and gaps in coverage. Doesn't cause a "high," thus it does not lead to abuse, and so a) it is not a controlled drug and b) may use with history of substance abuse.	Use cautiously in patients with hypertension, tachycardia, or cardiovascular or cerebrovascular disease because it can increase blood pressure and heart rate. Has some drug interactions. While extensively tested, short duration of population use.

.This chart was updated 6/15/05. Consult with your physician before making any decision regarding medication usage

DRUG	FORM	DOSING	SIDE EFFECTS	DURATION	PROS	PRECAUTIONS
BUPROPION						
WELLBUTRIN IR	Short Acting Tablet IR-75 mg 100 mg	Starting dose is 37.5 mg increasing gradually (wait at least 3 days) to maximum of 2-3 doses, no more than 150 mg/dose.	Irritability, decreased appetite, and insomnia.	About 4-6 hours.	Helpful for ADHD patients with comorbid depression or anxiety. May help after school until home.	Not indicated in patients with a seizure disorder or with a current or previous diagnosis of bulimia or anorexia. May worsen tics. May cause mood deterioration at the time it wears off.
WELLBUTRIN SR	Long Acting Tablet SR-100 mg 150mg 200mg	Starting dose is 100 mg/ day increasing gradually to a maximum of 2 doses, no more than 200 mg/ dose.	Same as Wellbutrin IR	About 10-14 hours.	Same for Wellbutrin IR. Lower seizure risk than immediate release form. Avoids noon dose.	Same as Wellbutrin IR. If a second dose is not given, may get mood deterioration at around 10-14 hours.
WELLBUTRIN XL	Long Acting Tablet 150mg 300mg	Starting dose is 150 mg /day increasing gradually to a maximum of 2 doses, no more than 300 mg/day.	Same as Wellbutrin IR	About 24 + hours.	Same for Wellbutrin IR. Single daily dose. Smooth 24 hour coverage. Lower seizure risk than immediate release form.	Same as Wellbutrin IR.
ALPHA-2 AGONISTS						
CATAPRES (clonidine)	Tablet 0.1 mg 0.2 mg 0.3 mg -------	Starting dose is .025 -.05 mg/ day in evening. Increase by similar dose every 7 days, adding to morning, mid-day, possibly afternoon, and again evening doses in sequence. Total dose of 0.1 -.3mg/day divided into 3-4 doses. Do not skip days.	Sleepiness, hypotension, headache, dizziness, stomachache, nausea, dry mouth, depression, nightmares.	Onset in 30-60 minutes. Duration about 3 - 6 hours.	Helpful for ADHD patients with comorbid tic disorder or insomnia. Good for severe impulsivity, hyperactivity and/or aggression. Stimulates appetite. Especially helpful in younger children (under 6) with ADHD symptoms associated with prenatal insult or syndrome such as Fragile X.	Sudden discontinuation could result in rebound hypertension. Minimize daytime tiredness by starting with evening dose and increasing slowly. Avoid brand and generic formulations with red dye, which may cause hyperarousal in sensitive children.
CLONIDINE	Tablet 0.1 mg 0.2 mg 0.3 mg					
CATAPRES Patch	TTS-1 TTS-2 TTS-3	Corresponds to doses of 0.1 mg, 0.2 mg and 0.3 mg per patch. (If using .1 mg tid tablets, try TTS 2 but likely need TTS 3).	Same as Catapres tablet but with skin patch there may be localized skin reactions.	Duration 4-5 days, so avoids the vacillations in drug effect seen in tablets.	Same as above.	Same as above. May get rebound hypertension and return of symptoms if it isn't recognized that a patch has come off or becomes loose. An immature student may get excessive dose from chewing on the patch.
TENEX (guanfacine) ------- guanfacine tablets	1 mg 2 mg 3 mg ------- 1 mg 2 mg 3 mg	Starting dose is 0.5 mg/day in evening and increase by similar dose every 7 days as indicated. Given in divided doses 2-4 times per day. Daily dose range 0.5 - 4mg/day. DO NOT skip days	Compared to clonidine, lower severity of side effects, especially fatigue and depression, less headache, stomache, nausea, dry mouth. Minimal problem of rebound hypertension if doses are missed.	Duration about 6 - 12 hours.	Can provide for 24/7 modulation of impulsivity, hyperactivity, aggression and sensory hypersensitivity. This covers most out of school problems, so stiumlant use can be limited to school and homework hours. Improves appetite. Less sedating than clonidine.	Avoid formulations with red dye as above. Hypotension is the primary dose-limiting problem. As with clonidine, important to check blood pressures with dose increases and if symptoms suggest hypotension, such as light-headedness.

This chart was updated 6/16/05. Consult with your physician before making any decision regarding medication usage.

difficulty falling asleep, irritable mood, and tics. These side effects are well understood in children.

Rebound. Some parents report that at the end of the school day, their child becomes more hyperactive, excitable, talkative, and irritable. This phenomena is referred to as "rebound," and it can affect many children with ADHD who take stimulant medication during the school day. When rebound occurs, it usually begins after the last dose of medication is wearing off. The doctor may recommend a smaller dose of medication be given or use of another medication to reduce the child's excitability. Rebound may be less common when using long-acting stimulants such as Ritalin LA, Concerta, Adderall XR, or Metadate CD.

Difficulty falling asleep. Children taking stimulants may have trouble falling asleep. They may be experiencing a drug rebound, which makes it difficult for them to quiet down and become restful. In some cases the doctor may recommend reducing or eliminating the mid-day dose of medication or may prescribe a small dose of stimulant medication before bedtime. You might try administering the medication earlier in the day so it is completely worn off by bedtime. If the child is taking a long-acting form of the medicine, try a short-acting form so that is completely worn off by bedtime. Other medications, such as Clonidine or Benadryl, may be prescribed to help the child fall asleep.

Non-medical interventions parents can try are: establish sleep routines in the home; avoid excessive activity or stimulation before bedtime; set a fixed bedtime and adhere to it; and teach the child how to relax in bed while trying to fall asleep.

Irritability. Clinicians and researchers both have noted that stimulant usage in ADHD children may worsen the child's mood. The child may exhibit more frequent temper outbursts, may become more moody and more easily frustrated than usual. Moodiness could lead to oppositional behavior at home. Stimulants can also produce dysphoria (sadness) in some children. If irritability, sadness, moodiness, or agitation become evident during the first one-two hours after the medication is taken the doctor may lower the dose. If irritability, sadness, moodiness, or agitation worsen as the medication wears off, your doctor may change to an extended-release form of the stimulant, overlap stimulant dosing (usually by thirty minutes), combine long- and short-acting forms, or consider using an additional medication. If irritability persists have the child assessed for depression and other psychiatric problems.

Tics and Tourette's syndrome. Simple motor tics consist of small, abrupt muscle movements usually around the face and upper body. Common simple motor tics include eye blinking, neck jerking, shoulder shrugging, and facial grimacing. Common simple vocal tics include throat clearing, grunting, sniffing, and snorting. Stimulants should be used with caution in patients with motor or vocal tics or in patients with a family history of tics. A little more than half of the ADHD children who start treatment with a stimulant medication will develop a subtle, transient motor or vocal tic. The tic might begin immediately or months after the medication is started. It might disappear on its own while the child is taking stimulants or it might worsen. Many physicians prefer to discontinue or reduce the stimulant medication if tics appear.

A child who has either a motor or a vocal tic (but not both), which occurs many times a day, nearly every day, for a period of at least one year (without stopping for more than three months) may be diagnosed as having a chronic tic disorder. Tourette's syndrome is a chronic tic disorder characterized by both multiple motor tics and one or more vocal tics. These tics are more severe than the simple motor tics described above. They involve the head and, frequently, other parts of the body such as the torso, arms, and legs. Vocal tics may include the production of sounds like clucking, grunting, yelping, barking, snorting, and coughing. Coprolalia, the utterance of obscenities, is rare and occurs in about ten percent of children with Tourette's. Stimulants should be used cautiously with children who have chronic tic disorder or Tourette's syndrome and ADHD as the medication may exacerbate the problem.

Cardiovascular effects and seizure threshold. There has been some speculation and concern that stimulant medications may produce adverse cardiovascular effects in children, particularly with long term use. While stimulants may cause some elevation of the heart rate in some children with ADHD, there is no evidence of any long term cardiovascular effects. Furthermore, there is no evidence that stimulants lower the seizure threshold putting the child at greater risk for having a seizure.

Abuse and dependency. There are no cases of methylphenidate abuse or dependence in the over hundreds of controlled studies of stimulants in children, adolescents, or adults with ADHD. Parents should not be overly concerned that the use of a stimulant medication would lead to dependence, addiction, or drug abuse. However, misuse/abuse of stimulants can and does occur and parents should be aware of this. There have been fairly frequent reports of elementary and secondary school children giving away or selling stimulants, reports of diversion of stimulants into the hands of family members and teachers, and attempts by people to secure stimulants through unlawful prescriptions. Parents should maintain possession of any stimulant medication at home and carefully monitor the supply. The school should do so as well for medication dispensed during the school day. Hopefully, use of long-acting stimulants given once a day will reduce this problem.

Non-Stimulants to Treat ADHD

There is no doubt that stimulants are safe and effective in the treatment of ADHD and that they are generally considered the first-line medication to use. However, not all children will show an adequate response to stimulants, some may develop adverse side effects, and others may benefit from a medication that has twenty-four hour effectiveness rather than the limited coverage that stimulants can provide. In addition, the fact that stimulants are controlled substances, worries some parents who would like an alternative medication.

Atomoxetine (Strattera) has been marketed for the past few years as an FDA approved treatment for ADHD in children and in adults. It is a selective norepinephrine reuptake inhibitor (SNRI) and as such it blocks the reuptake of norepinephrine in certain regions of the brain. It is administered in the morning (or at night if the child becomes too sedated) and the dose is based on body weight. The starting dose is 0.5 mg/kg and the target daily dose might be 1.2 mg/kg. Strattera comes in capsules of 10, 18, 25, 40, and 60 mg strengths. It could take four to six weeks (or more) to reach maximal effect, however, the effects last twenty-four hours a day. It is sometimes used in combination with stimulants. In children, the side effects most likely to be seen with Strattera include stomach aches, sedation, nausea and vomiting, loss of appetite and headaches.

Tricyclic Antidepressants

Tricyclic antidepressants (TCAs) are primarily used in children for ADHD and tic disorders. They are regarded as alternatives for children who have not succeeded with stimulants, for whom stimulants produced unacceptable side effects, or who suffer from other conditions (such as depression, anxiety, Tourette's syndrome, tics), or aggressive behavior and irritability along with ADHD. Imipramine (Tofranil), desipramine (Norpramin), amytriptyline (Elavil), and nortriptyline (Pamelor or Vivactyl), doxepin, and clomipramine (Anafranil) are TCAs.

TCAs have the advantage of longer duration of action (all day) as opposed to four to twelve hours common to stimulants. This avoids the troublesome and even embarrassing mid-day stimulant dose taken at school. Unfortunately, TCAs may not be as effective as the stimulants in improving attention and concentration or reducing hyperactive-impulsive symptoms of ADHD. TCAs also can produce adverse side effects, the most common of which are drowsiness, dry mouth, constipation, and abdominal discomfort. More concern, however, has been expressed at possible adverse cardiac side effects, accidental overdose, and build up in the body to potentially lethal levels. By drawing blood, levels of the TCA can be measured to determine whether these symptoms are a result of too much medication in the body or other factors related to the child's illness.

Antihypertensives

Antihypertensive agents such as clonidine (Catapres) and guanfacine (Tenex) have been found to be useful in the treatment of ADHD children, especially those who are extremely hyperactive, excitable, impulsive, and defiant. They have less effectiveness in improving attention. These drugs are also frequently used in to treat Tourette's disorder and other tic disorders and they help control aggression in children with autism and pervasive developmental disorder. Clonidine is also prescribed to help children who have difficulty falling asleep. It can be a great benefit to children with sleep onset difficulties whether the cause is ADHD overarousal, stimulant medication rebound, or unwillingness to fall asleep. Clonidine works on the adrenergic chemical system in the brain and affects the release of norepinephrine.

Clonidine is a relatively short-acting drug as it works for about four hours in children so multiple doses are needed. It comes in a tablet form or in a skin patch. The skin patch may be useful to improve compliance and provide more even absorption in the body. Sudden discontinuation of this medication can cause increased hyperactivity, headache, agitation, elevated blood pressure and pulse, and an increase in tics in patients with Tourette's syndrome. Sleepiness, which is the most common side effect of clonidine, gradually decreases after a few weeks. Other side effects may include dry mouth, dizziness, nausea, irritability, and light sensitivity. The skin patch can cause a rash.

Clonidine may be combined with stimulants for children with severe hyperactivity and aggression, for children with tic disorders and ADHD, or sleep problems in children with ADHD.

Guanfacine is a long-acting noradrenergic agonist similar to clonidine in effect, but it has a longer duration of action and less side-effects. It is used with children who cannot tolerate the sedative effects of clonidine or with children for whom the effects of clonidine were too short.

Antidepressants

Selective serotonin reuptake inhibitors (SSRIs) are the most commonly used antidepressants for children. These include fluoxetine (Prozac), paroxetine (Paxil), citalopram (Celexa), sertraline (Zoloft), escitalopram (Lexapro), and fluvoxamine (Luvox). These drugs have not been well studied in the treatment of ADHD. SSRIs have, however, gained considerable recognition for treatment of depression, anxiety, and obsessive-compulsive disorders. They are considered the first line of medication treatment for these conditions. They have fewer sedative, cardiovascular, and weight-gain side effects than other antidepressants. The SSRIs are similar in their overall effect of making serotonin available in certain regions of the brain, but they vary somewhat from one another in their chemical make-up. Therefore, when one SSRI proves ineffective for a child, another may be more effective. Parents should be cautious however, about the use of antidepressants in general (including the SSRIs) in children. In October 2003 the FDA issued a health advisory warning doctors to exercise caution in prescribing the SSRIs for children and adolescents and to closely monitor those who take these medications. There are concerns that the SSRIs may increase suicidal ideation or suicide attempts in children and adolescents.

Bupropion (Wellbutrin) is a novel antidepressant drug that has been used successfully for a number of years to treat ADHD. It has not been well studied in this regard, but clinicians using this medication find it has a place in treating ADHD, especially in children who do not tolerate stimulants or who may have co-existing problems with mood. Bupropion appears to possess both indirect dopamine and noradrenergic effects. It works rapidly, peaking in the blood after two hours and lasting up to fourteen hours. The usual dose range in children is from 37.5 to 300 mg per day in two or three divided doses. There is a sustained-release preparation (100, 150, and 200 mg) that can be given once or twice daily. An extended-release form (150 mg and 300 mg) can be given once in the morning. The major side-effects in children are irritability, decreased appetite, insomnia, and worsening of tics. Irritability can be reduced with decreased dosing. Bupropion may worsen tics and should not be used when a seizure disorder is suspected.

Venlafaxine (Effexor) is an antidepressant that, like SSRIs, enhances serotonin in certain areas of the brain by blocking its reuptake, but it also possesses some noradrenergic properties. For this reason it is known as an SNRI (serotonin-norepinephrine reuptake inhibitor). It can improve symptoms of ADHD and is also helpful for depression in children. The usual dose range is 12.5 mg up to a total of 225 mg daily in twice-a-day split dosing. An extended-release (XR) tablet is available allowing once-a-day dosing. Side effects can include nausea, agitation, stomachaches, headaches, and, at higher doses, blood pressure elevation. As with other anti-depressants, there may be a greater risk of suicidally in children and therefore, careful observation of your child while starting this treatment and during the earlier phases of treatment is very important.

Buspirone, an anxiolitic medication, has been used in children and adolescents with anxiety disorders and researchers have reported significant improvement with it. It has not been well studied in the treatment of ADHD in children

Fenfluramine, benzodiazepines, or lithium are of benefit in other psychiatric disorders, but there is no support to their use in the treatment of ADHD.

Antipsychotics
The group of medications called antipsychotics are commonly used to treat disorders other than psychosis and have been found to be very helpful in children who have severe mood lability. They include haloperidol (Haldol), pimozide (Orap), thioridazine (Mellaril), chlorpromazine (Thorazine), and others. They are frequently prescribed to children with severe mood disorders when other medications have failed. Because they have serious side effects, they are reserved for children who show severe problems and who don't respond to other medications. Common short-term, reversible side effects are drowsiness, increased appetite and weight gain, dizziness, dry mouth, congestion, and blurred vision. Some of the anti-psychotic drugs can produce side effects that affect various muscle groups (extrapyramidal effects) leading to muscle tightness and spasm, rolling eyes, and restlessness. Some of these severe side effects may be reduced by using the newer, atypical antipsychotics.

Atypical Antipsychotics
This class of medication includes ziprasidone (Geodon), aripiprazole (Abilify), risperidone (Risperdal), clozapine (Clozaril), olanzapine (Zyprexa), and quetiapine (Seroquel). They are increasingly being used as first-line drugs for children with severe mood disorders, disruptive disorders, self-injurious behavior, bipolar disorder, and psychosis. These drugs affect the dopamine system and have less severe side-effects than the traditional antipsychotics. Side effects of Risperdal, Zyprexa, and Seroquel appear similar to those of the traditional antipsychotics, but the rate of side effects and the risk of long-term tardive dyskinesia (irreversible motor writing/twitches/spasms) seem to be much lower. One of the most problematic long-term effects of some of the atypical antipsychotics (particularly Zyprexa and to a lesser extent, Risperdal), is

weight gain and potential effects on metabolism. It is unclear whether Seroquel or Geodon have these problems. Abilify does not appear to cause increased weight, but may cause motor spasms that may result in a greater risk for tardive dyskinesia with prolonged use.

Sticking with Medication

ADHD is a chronic condition with symptoms that persist throughout childhood and adolescence. Therefore, children receiving medical treatment may have to continue such treatment for years depending on the severity of their symptoms. The presence of co-morbid conditions such as oppositional defiant disorder, conduct disorder, or anxiety and mood disorders make it even more important that medical treatments be adhered to. However, parents may worry about the long-term effects of continuously dispensing ADHD medication to their child. Anxious children may also worry about taking the medication. Children with oppositional defiant disorder often refuse to take medication. And older children and adolescence tend to dislike taking medication. Because of these factors, adherence to medication treatment is an ongoing process. Children may discontinue medication over time, but children may also restart medication after varying lengths of time. It is important to maintain an open mind about the risks and benefits of medication over the course of the child's development.

Summary

Medications are commonly used to treat people of all ages who have ADHD. We used to think ADHD medications were a treatment of last resort, only to be used after other treatments have been tried and failed, or in children and adolescents who are most severely affected. This is no longer the case. The use of medication is common, generally safe, and very effective for the treatment of ADHD. Results of many controlled studies indicated that medication alone can be very effective to reduce core symptoms of ADHD if dosing is carefully adjusted and monitored.

There are several classes of medications used in the treatment of ADHD. Stimulants are the most frequently used and antidepressants and anti-hypertensives are less often prescribed. There have been many controlled studies of stimulants in the treatment of ADHD. These studies confirm their effectiveness in more than seventy percent of children with improvements noted in attention, activity level, impulsivity, work completion in school, and compliant behavior. New, long-acting stimulants, which can last ten to twelve hours, will eliminate the need for mid-day dosing and may reduce rebound effects.

Antidepressants have been less well studied, but are useful in treating adolescents who do not respond well to the stimulants or who are suffering from depression or low self-esteem in addition to ADHD. The antihypertensive medications have also been less well studied than stimulants and are used to treat those with ADHD who may be very hyperactive, who are aggressive, or who have an accompanying tic disorder. New medications are being tested for treatment of ADHD with some promising results.

When medications are used in treatment, their effects should be monitored. Adjustments in dosage, time taken, or changes in medication type may be made by the physician if problems arise. Parents, teachers, and the adolescent taking the medication should each be responsible for communicating medication effects.

Medication will rarely be the only treatment a child, adolescent, or adult with ADHD receives. A multi-modal treatment program should be considered including counseling, education about ADHD, and school-based or work-based accommodations and interventions.

Appendix*

ADHD Symptom Checklist

Positive Reinforcement Worksheet

Giving Clear Instructions Worksheet

Using Time-Out Worksheet

Standing Rules Worksheet

Home Behavior Chart

Daily Report Cards

Sorting Out Behaviors Worksheet

* Appendix pages may be reproduced for personal use.

ADHD Symptom Checklist

Below is a checklist containing the eighteen symptoms of ADHD. Items 1-9 describe characteristics of inattention. Items 10-15 describe characteristics of hyperactivity. Items 16-18 describe characteristics of impulsivity. In the space before each statement, put the number that best describes your child's behavior (0=never or rarely; 1 = sometimes; 2 = often; 3 = very often).

Inattention Symptoms

____ 1. Fails to give close attention to details or makes careless mistakes in schoolwork, work, or other activities.

____ 2. Has difficulty sustaining attention in tasks or play activities.

____ 3. Does not seem to listen when spoken to directly.

____ 4. Does not follow through on instructions and fails to finish schoolwork, chores, or duties in the workplace (not due to oppositional behavior or failure to understand instructions).

____ 5. Has difficulty organizing tasks and activities.

____ 6. Avoids, dislikes, or is reluctant to engage in tasks that require sustained mental effort (such as schoolwork or homework).

____ 7. Loses things necessary for tasks or activities (e.g., toys, school assignments, pencils, books, or tools).

____ 8. Is easily distracted by extraneous stimuli.

____ 9. Is often forgetful in daily activities.

Hyperactive-Impulsive Symptoms

____ 10. Fidgets with hands or feet or squirms in seat.

____ 11. Leaves seat in classroom or in other situations in which remaining seated is expected.

____ 12. Runs about or climbs excessively in situations in which it is inappropriate (in adolescents or adults, may be limited to subjective feelings of restlessness).

____ 13. Has difficulty playing or engaging in leisure activities quietly.

____ 14. Is "on the go" or often acts as if "driven by a motor."

____ 15. Talks excessively.

____ 16. Blurts out answers before questions have been completed.

____ 17. Has difficulty awaiting his or her turn.

____ 18. Interrupts or intrudes on others (e.g., butts into conversations or games).

Count the number of items in each group (inattention items 1-9 and hyperactivity-impulsivity items 10-18) you marked "2" or "3." If six or more items are marked "2" or "3" in each group this could indicate serious problems in the groups marked.

Using Positive Reinforcement Worksheet

This worksheet is designed to help parents recognize how they have been using positive reinforcement to manage their child's misbehavior and to practice doing so.

Step 1: Think Positive
List several ways in which you provide positive reinforcement to your child for behaving appropriately. Put a check mark next to the reinforcers that you think are most effective in strengthening your child's positive behavior.
A. Example: Verbal praise such as "You're a great listener."
B. Example: Bragging to others about the child in earshot of the child.

1. _____
2. _____
3. _____
4. _____
5. _____

Step 2: Identify Two Target Behavior To Reinforce
Fill in the item below with two target behaviors that you would like your child to exhibit more often (as in the example below).
Target Behavior to Reinforce:
A. Example: Sitting down and doing homework by himself in room and working for twenty minutes.

1. _____
2. _____

Step 3: Plan Your Reinforcement
Write down exactly how you plan to reinforce your child each time the target behaviors listed above are done.
Everytime my child _____
I will reinforce him/her by_____

Step 4: Reinforce Immediately and Continuously
When strengthening a new behavior it is best at first to reinforce immediately and frequently. Remind yourself to look for the target behavior or behavior that resembles the target behavior and immediately deliver the reinforcement. Catch the child being good.

Step 5: Keep Track of Your Child's Success
Create a chart at home for the target behavior you want your child to exhibit more often and provide stickers, happy faces, etc., as reinforcement. Provide an incentive for good performance on the chart.

Giving Clear Instructions Worksheet

Follow these steps when giving a command.
1. Get the child's attention.
2. Move close to the child.
3. Say the child's name.
4. Establish eye contact.
5. State the command clearly in a firm voice.
6. Use a "do" command rather than a "stop" command when you can. For example, "Please put the game away now!" versus "Stop fooling around!"
7. Provide any explanation before stating the command, not after.
8. Wait five seconds.
9. Do not talk to the child during this time.
10. Do not walk away or look away.

If the child starts to comply:
1. Pay attention as the child begins to execute the command.
2. Praise or reward the child when the command has been performed correctly.

If the child does not begin to comply within 5 seconds.
1. Issue a warning as an "If…then" statement that specifies the desired behavior and the consequences for noncompliance (e.g., "If you don't put away the game, then you will have to go to time-out."
2. Allow five more seconds for compliance.
3. If the child complies the parent continues to pay attention and provides praise.
4. If the child does not comply the parent follows through on the previous warning.

Using Time-out Worksheet

This worksheet is designed to give parents structured practice in using the time-out.

Step 1: Identify Target Behaviors

Complete the list below with specific target misbehaviors that you will consequate with time-out and the opposite appropriate behaviors that you will positively reinforce with a specific reinforcer.

Misbehaviors To Time-out

A. Example: Interrupting parents during conversation.

1. _____
2. _____

Appropriate Behaviors To Reinforce

A. Example: Praise for not interrupting during parents' conversation.

1. _____
2. _____

Step 2: Choose A Time-out Place

The time-out place will be_____.

Step 3: Decide On The Length Of Time-out.

Time-out will last _____ minutes for each of the above misbehaviors.

Step 4: Time-out Enforcement Checklist

- Get near the child and immediately instruct the child to stop the misbehavior.
- Warn the child that if he does not listen he will go to time-out.
- Wait five seconds and if the child does not comply send him to time-out.
- Don't explain, criticize, or lecture.
- Threaten the child with backup consequences such as removal of other privileges if the child refuses to stay in time-out.
- Use a timer to keep track of when time-out is over.
- After time-out is served have the child state what he did wrong and apologize.

Step 5 : Keep Track Of The Target Misbehavior

This step requires you to keep track of your progress. For each of the target misbehaviors listed under Step 1, record the number of times per day the child exhibited each misbehavior. Remember, the child should receive a time-out every time he does not listen to your instruction first and then your warning to stop the misbehavior. By keeping track of the number of times each misbehavior occurs over a few days, you should be able to determine if time-out is being effective in decreasing the misbehavior.

Standing Rules Worksheet

Write five standing rules that you will explain to your child. Include a consequence that will occur if a rule is broken. Post these standing rules in at least two places in the house.

1.

2.

3.

4.

5.

Home Behavior Chart

START BEHAVIORS	Value	Su	Mo	Tu	We	Th	Fr	Sa
1								
2								
3								
4								
5								
6								
7 Extra Credit!								
TOTAL TOKENS EARNED								

STOP BEHAVIORS	Value	Su	Mo	Tu	We	Th	Fr	Sa
1								
2								
3								
4								
5								
6								
7 Extra Penalty								
TOTAL TOKENS LOST (Minus)								

TOTAL TOKENS AVAILABLE								

REWARDS/PRIVILEGES	Value	Su	Mo	Tu	We	Th	Fr	Sa
1								
2								
3								
4								
5								
6								
7								
8								
TOTAL TOKENS SPENT								

TOTAL TOKENS REMAINING								

Daily Report Card
Rating By Day

Instructions: Please use the report card for one week. Evaluate the student's daily performance on each behavior listed below. Using the guide below, write a number in each space that indicates the student's performance in that area for the day. Use the space at the bottom for daily comments.

Name_____   Grade_____

Teacher_____   Week of _____

Days of the Week	MON	TUE	WED	THU	FRI
Behaviors:					
1. Paid attention in class	____	____	____	____	____
2. Completed work in class	____	____	____	____	____
3. Completed homework	____	____	____	____	____
4. Was well behaved	____	____	____	____	____
5. Desk and notebook neat	____	____	____	____	____
TOTALS	____	____	____	____	____

Teacher's Initials

5 = Excellent
4 = Good
3 = Fair
2 = Needs Improvement
1 = Poor
N/A = not applicable

Teacher's Comments

Parent's Comments

Daily Report Card
Rating By Day

Instructions: Please use the report card for one week. Evaluate the student's daily performance on each behavior listed below (parent or teacher insert). Using the guide below, write a number in each space that indicates the student's performance in that area for the day. Use the space at the bottom for daily comments.

Name_____   Grade_____

Teacher_____   Week of _____

Days of the Week	MON	TUE	WED	THU	FRI
Behaviors					
1. _____	____	____	____	____	____
2. _____	____	____	____	____	____
3. _____	____	____	____	____	____
4. _____	____	____	____	____	____
5. _____	____	____	____	____	____
TOTALS	____	____	____	____	____

Teacher's Initials

5 = Excellent
4 = Good
3 = Fair
2 = Needs Improvement
1 = Poor
N/A = not applicable

Teacher's Comments

Parent's Comments

Daily Report Card
Rating By Subject

Instructions: Please use the report card for one day. Evaluate the student's performance on each behavior listed below. Using the guide below, write a number in each space that indicates the student's performance in each subject for the day. Use the space at the bottom for daily comments.

Name_____   Grade_____

Teacher_____   Week of _____

Subject: ____ ____ ____ ____ ____

Behaviors:

1. Paid attention in class   ____ ____ ____ ____ ____

2. Completed work in class   ____ ____ ____ ____ ____

3. Completed homework   ____ ____ ____ ____ ____

4. Was well behaved   ____ ____ ____ ____ ____

5. Desk and notebook neat   ____ ____ ____ ____ ____

TOTALS   ____ ____ ____ ____ ____

Teacher's Initials
5= Excellent
4= Good
3 = Fair
2 = Needs Improvement
1 = Poor
N/A = not applicable

Teacher's Comments

Parent's Comments

Daily Report Card
Rating By Subject

Instructions: Please use the report card for one day. Evaluate the student's performance on each behavior listed below (parent or teacher insert). Using the guide below, write a number in each space that indicates the student's performance in each subject for the day. Use the space at the bottom for daily comments.

Name_____   Grade_____

Teacher_____   Week of _____

Subject: ____ ____ ____ ____ ____

Behaviors

1. _____   ____ ____ ____ ____ ____

2. _____   ____ ____ ____ ____ ____

3. _____   ____ ____ ____ ____ ____

4. _____   ____ ____ ____ ____ ____

5. _____   ____ ____ ____ ____ ____

TOTALS   ____ ____ ____ ____ ____

Teacher's Initials

5 = Excellent

4 = Good

3 = Fair

2 = Needs Improvement

1 = Poor

N/A = not applicable

Teacher's Comments

Parent's Comments

Sorting Out Behaviors Worksheet

Consider the Collaborative Problem Solving approach to managing behavior that is discussed in Chapter 6. Take a look at the following behaviors and check the basket you want to put them in using the guide below. Think about how you might respond to each behavior based on which basket you selected. Ask another adult to do this and compare your responses.

Basket A contains behaviors that are very very important and worth risking a "meltdown" over.
Basket B contains behaviors that are somewhat important and need to be talked about.
Basket C contains behaviors that are not that important and can be ignored.

	A	**B**	**C**
1. crossing the street without looking	___	___	___
2. leaving shoes in the living room	___	___	___
3. dawdling in the morning instead of getting ready for school	___	___	___
4. throwing a rock at younger brother	___	___	___
5. refusing to get started on homework right after school	___	___	___
6. talking back to mother	___	___	___
7. calling sister a name	___	___	___
8. arguing at the dinner table	___	___	___
9. refusing to stay in time-out	___	___	___
10. not starting homework at the scheduled time	___	___	___

List other behaviors your child exhibits and check the basket that is appropriate to guide your response for each behavior.

	A	**B**	**C**
_____	___	___	___
_____	___	___	___
_____	___	___	___
_____	___	___	___

References and Resources

References

American Psychiatric Association (2000). *Diagnostic and Statistical Manual of Mental Disorders, Fourth Edition, Text Revision.* Washington, DC: American Psychiatric Press.

Angold, A., Erkanli, A., Egger, H.L., & Costello, E.J. Stimulant treatment for children: A community perspective. (2000). *Journal of the American Academy of Child and Adolescent Psychiatry*, 39, 975-984.

Barkley, R. A. (2001). *Taking Charge of ADHD: The Complete, Authoritative Guide for Parents (2nd edition).* New York: Guilford Press.

Barkley, R. A. (1998). *Attention-Deficit Hyperactivity Disorder: Handbook for Diagnosis and Treatment.* New York: Guilford Press.

Barkley, R. A. (1997). *Defiant Children. A Clinician's Manual for Assessment and Parent Training.* New York: Guilford Press.

Biederman, J., Faraone, S., Mick, E., Williamson, S., Wilens, T., Spencer, T., Weber, W., Jetton J., Draus, I., Pert, J., & Allen, B. (1999). Clinical correlates of ADHD in females: Findings from a large group of girls ascertained from pediatric and psychiatric referral sources. *Journal of the American Academy of Child and Adolescent Psychiatry*, 38, 966-975.

Campbell, S. B. (1990). *Behavior Problems in Preschool Children.* New York: Guilford Press.

Casey, B.J., Castellanos, F.X., Giedd, J.N., Marsh, W.L., Hamburger, S.D., Schubert, A.B., Vauss, Y.C., Vaituzis, A.C., Dickstein, D.P., Sarfatti, S.E., & Rapaport, J.L.. (1997). Implications of right frontostriatal circuitry in response inhibition and attention deficit/ hyperactivity disorder. *Journal of the American Academy of Child and Adolescent Psychiatry*, 36, 374-383.

Castellanos, D.Z. (1997). Toward a pathophysiology of attention-deficit/hyperactivity disorder. *Clinical Pediatrics*, 36, 381-393.

Conners, K. (2001). *Feeding the Brain: How Foods Affect Children.* Plenum, New York.

Cook, E. H., Jr., Stein, M.A., Krasowski, M.D., Cox, N.J., Olkon, D.M., Kieffer, J.E., & Leventhal, B. L. (1995). Association of attention-deficit disorder and the dopamine transporter gene. *American Journal of Human Genetics*, 56, 993-998.

DuPaul, G.J., McGoey, K.E., Eckert, T.L., & VanBrakle, J. (2001). Preschool children with attention-deficit/hyperactivity disorder: Impairments in behavioral, social, and school functioning. *Journal of the American Academy of Child and Adolescent Psychiatry*, 40, 508-515.

Faraone, S.V. & Biederman, J. (1994). Is attention deficit hyperactivity disorder familial? *Harvard Review of Psychiatry*, 1, 271-287.

Faraone, S., Biederman, J., Keenan, K., & Tsuang, M. (1991). A family-genetic study of girls with DSM-III attention deficit disorder. *American Journal of Psychiatry*, 148 (1), 112-115.

Filipek, P.A., Semrud-Clikeman, M., Steingard, R.J., Renshaw, P.F., Kennedy, D.N., & Biederman, J. (1997). Volumetric MRI analysis comparing subjects having attention-deficit hyperactivity disorder with normal controls. *Neurology*, 48, 589-601.

Goldstein, S. (2002). *Understanding, Diagnosing, and Treating ADHD Through the Lifespan.* Florida: Specialty Press, Inc.

Greene, Ross. (2001). *The Explosive Child: A New Approach for Understanding and Parenting Easily Frustrated, Chronically Inflexible Children.* New York: HarperCollins Publishers.

Hinshaw, S., Carte, E., Sami, N., Treuting, J., & Zupan, B. (2002). Preadolescent girls with attention-deficit/hyperactivity disorder: II. Neuropsychological performance in relation to subtypes and individual classification. *Journal of Consulting & Clinical Psychology*, 70(5), 1099-1111.

Hynd, G. W., Semrud-Clikeman, M., Lorys. A.R., Novey, E.S., Elopulos, D., & Lytinen, H.

(1991). Corpus callosum morphology in attention deficit-hyperactivity disorder: Morphometric analysis of MRI. *Journal of Learning Disabilities,* 24, 141-146.

Jacobsen, B. & Kinney, D.K. (1980). Perinatal complications in adopted and non-adopted schizophrenics and their controls: preliminary result. *Acta Psychiatrica Scandinavica Supplement,* 285, 337-346.

Jensen, P.S., Bhatara, V.S., Vitiello, B., Hoagwood, K., Feil, M., & Burke, L. (1999) Psychoactive medication prescribing practices for U.S. children: gaps between research and clinical practice. *Journal of the American Academy of Child and Adolescent Psychiatry,* 38, 557-565

LaHoste, G.J., Swanson, J.M., Wigal, S.B., Glabe, C., Wigal, T., King, N., & Kennedy, J.L. (1996). Dopamine D4 receptor gene polymorphism is associated with attention deficit hyperactivity disorder. *Molecular Psychiatry,* 1, 121-124.

Lavigne J.V., Arend R., et al. (1998). Psychiatric disorders With Onset in the Preschool Years: I. Stability of Diagnosis. *Journal of the American Academy of Child and Adolescent Psychiatry,* 37,1246–1254

Levy, F., Hay, D.A., McStephen, M.D., Wood, C. & Waldman, I. (1997). Attention-deficit hyperactivity disorder: a category or a continuum? Genetic analysis of a large-scale twin study. *Journal of the American Academy of Child and Adolescent Psychiatry,* 36, 737-744.

Levy, R., O'Hanlon, B., & Goode, T.N. (2001). *Try and Make Me! Simple Strategies That Turn Off the Tantrums and Create Cooperation.* Emmaus, PA: Rodale.

Levy, R. and Smith, K. (2004). *I've Had It With You.* Dallas, TX: Effective Behavior Solutions.

McMahon, R., & Forehand, R. (2003). *Helping the Noncompliant Child.* (2nd edition). Guilford Press: New York.

Murphy, K. & Barkley, R.A. (1996). Prevalence of DSM-IV symptoms of ADHD in adult licensed drivers: Implications for clinical diagnosis. *Journal of Attention Disorders,* 1, 147-161.

Nadeau, K., Littman, E., & Quinn, P. (2000). *Understanding Girls with AD/HD.* Silver Spring, MD: Advantage Books.

Needleman, H.L. (1998). Childhood lead poisoning: the promise and abandonment of primary prevention. *American Journal of Public Health,* 88, 1871-1877.

Phelan, T. (2003). *1-2-3 Magic: Effective Discipline for Children 2-12 (3rd Edition).* Glen Ellyn, Illinois: ParentMagic, Inc.

Rief, S. F. (2005). *How to Reach and Teach Children with ADD/ADHD. (2nd Edition).* New York: Jossey Bass.

Simpson, G.A., Bloom, B., Cohen, R.A., Blumberg, S., & Bourdon, K.H. (2005). U.S. Children with Emotional and Behavioral Difficulties: Data from the 2001, 2002, and 2003 National Health Interview Surveys. Advance data from vital and health statistics; No. 360. Hyattsville, MD: National Center for Health Statistics.

Sirotowitz, S., Davis, L., & Parker, H. (2004). *Study Strategies for Early School Success.* Plantation, FL: Specialty Press.

Weiss, G., & Hechtman, L. T. (1993). *Hyperactive Children Grown Up. (2nd edition).* New York: Guilford Press.

Wilens, T.E. (2004). *Straight Talk About Psychiatric Medications for Kids. (2nd Edition).* New York: Guilford Press.

Yeates, K.O., Armstrong, K, Janusz, J, Taylor, H.G., Wade, S, Stancin, T.,& Drotar, D. (2005). Long-term attention problems in children with traumatic brain Injury. *Journal of the American Academy of Child and Adolescent Psychiatry*, 44, 574-583.

Zentall, S., & S. Goldstein. (1998). *Seven Steps to Homework Success: A Family Guide for Solving Common Homework Problems.* Plantation, FL: Specialty Press.

Recommended Reading

Adamec, C. (2000). *Moms with ADD: A Self Help Manual.* Dallas, Texas: Taylor Trade Publishing.

Barkley, R. A. (2001). *Taking Charge of ADHD: The Complete, Authoritative Guide for Parents (2nd edition).* New York: Guilford Press.

Barkley, R. A. (1998). *Your Defiant Child: Eight Steps to Better Behavior.* New York: Guilford.

Clark, L. (1996). *SOS: Help for Parents (2nd edition).* Bowling Green, KY: Parents Press.

Goldstein, S. & Mathers, N. (1998). *Overcoming underachievement: An action guide to helping your child succeed in school.* New York: John Wiley & Sons.

Heininger, J., & Weiss, S.K. (2001). *From Chaos to Calm: Effective Parenting of Challenging Children with ADHD and Other Behavioral Problems.* New York: Perigree Books.

Kilcarr, P. J., & Quinn, P. (1997). *Voices from Fatherhood.* New York: Brunner-Mazel.

Koplewicz, H. S. (1996). *It's Nobody's Fault: New Hope and Help for Difficult Children and Their Parents.* New York: Random House.

Levy, R., O'Hanlon, B., & Goode, T.N. (2001). *Try and Make Me! Simple Strategies That Turn Off the Tantrums and Create Cooperation.* Emmaus, PA: Rodale.

Nadeau, K., Littman, E., & Quinn, P. (2000). *Understanding Girls with AD/HD.* Silver Spring, MD: Advantage Books.

Novotni, M. (1999). *What Does Everyone Else Know That I Don't: Social Skills Help for Adults with Attention Deficit/Hyperactivity Disorder (AD/HD).* Florida: Specialty Press, Inc.

Parker, H.C. (2001). *Problem Solver Guide for Students with ADHD.* Florida: Specialty Press, Inc.

Parker, H.C. (1992). *ADAPT: Attention Deficit Accommodation Plan for Teaching.* Plantation, FL: Specialty Press, Inc.

Phelan, T. (2003). *1-2-3 Magic: Effective Discipline for Children 2-12 (3rd Edition).* Glen Ellyn, Illinois: ParentMagic, Inc.

Phelan, T. W. (1998). *Surviving Your Adolescents: How to Manage and Let Go of Your 13-18 Year Olds.* Glen Ellyn, IL: Child Management Press.

Rief, S. F. (2005). *How to Reach and Teach Children with ADD/ADHD. (2nd Edition).* New York: Jossey Bass.

Rief, S. F. (1998). *The ADD/ADHD Checklist: An Easy Reference for Parents and Teachers.* New York: Simon and Schuster.

Sirotowitz, S., Davis, L., & Parker, H. (2004). *Study Strategies for Early School Success.* Plantation, FL: Specialty Press.

Zentall, S., & Goldstein, S. (1998). *Seven Steps to Homework Success: A Family Guide for Solving Common Homework Problems.* Plantation, FL: Specialty Press.

Video and Audio Programs

Barkley, R. A. (1992). *ADHD—What do we know?* New York: The Guilford Press.

Barkley, R. A. (1992). *ADHD—What can we do?* New York: The Guilford Press.

Levy, R. & Smith, K. (2004). *I've Had it With You.* Dallas, Tx: Effective Behavior Solutions.

Online Resources

Attention Deficit Disorder Association
www.add.org
Articles and resources about ADHD in Adults

ADDitude Magazine
www.additudemag.com
Articles about ADHD

ADD WareHouse
www.addwarehouse.com
Books, videos, and assessment products on ADHD and related disorders.

Children and Adults with Attention-Deficit/Hyperactivity Disorder
www.chadd.org
Articles and resources about ADHD across the lifespan

Sam Goldstein, Ph.D.
www.samgoldstein.com
Articles and resources about childhood and adult conditions

Learning Disabilities Association of America
www.ldanatl.org
Articles and resources about learning disabilities across the lifespan

MyADHD.com
www.myadhd.com
Articles and resources about ADHD including assessment tools, tracking tools, and treatment tools.

Support Groups and Associations

American Occupational Therapy Association
4720 Montgomery Lane
Bethesda, MD 20814
(301) 652-2682
www.aota.org

American Speech-Language-Hearing Association
10801 Rockville Pike
Rockville, MD 20852
(800) 638-8255
www.asha.org

Association on Higher Education and Disability (AHEAD)
P.O. Box 21192
Columbus, OH 43221-0192
(614) 488-4972

Attention Deficit Disorders Association (ADDA)
P.O. Box 543
Pottstown, PA 19464
Phone: 484-945-2101
www.adda.org

Children and Adults with Attention Deficit Hyperactivity Disorder (CHADD)
8181 Professional Drive, Suite 202
Lanham, MD 20706
(800) 233-4050
www.chadd.org

Council for Exceptional Children
Eric Clearinghouse on Disabilities and Education
1920 Association Drive
Reston, VA 20191
(800) 328-0272
www.cec.sped.org

Learning Disabilities Association of America (LDAA)
4156 Library Road
Pittsburgh, PA 15234
(412) 341-1515
www.ldanatl.org

National Information Center for Children and Youth with Disabilities (NICHCY)
P.O. Box 1492
Washington, DC 20013-1492
(800) 695-0285
www.nichcy.org

Recordings for the Blind and Dyslexic
20 Roszel Road
Princeton, NJ 08540
(800) 221-4792

Tourette Syndrome Association
4240 Bell Blvd.
Bayside, NY 11361
(718) 224-2999

Resources for Books, Videos, Training, and Assessment Products

A.D.D. WareHouse
300 N. W. 70th Ave., Suite 102
Plantation, Florida 33317
(800) 233-9273 • (954) 792-8100
www.addwarehouse.com

American Guidance Service
4201 Woodland Road
Circle Pines, MN 55014
(800) 328-2560
www.agsnet.com

Boys Town Press
14100 Crawford Street
Boys Town, NE 68010
(800) 282-6657
www.ffbh.boystown.org

Educational Resource Specialists
P.O. Box 19207
San Diego, CA 92159
(800) 682-3528

Franklin Electronic Publishers Inc.
One Franklin Plaza
Burlington, NJ 08016
(800) 525-9673

Free Spirit Publishing
400 First Ave. North, Suite 616
Minneapolis, MN 55401
(800) 735-7323
www.freespirit.com

Gordon Systems, Inc.
P.O. Box 746
DeWitt, N.Y. 13214-746
(315) 446-4849

Guilford Publications
72 Spring St.
New York, New York, 10012
(800) 365-7006
www.guilford.com

Hawthorne Educational Services
800 Gray Oak Drive
Columbia, MO 65201
(800) 542-1673

MHS
908 Niagara Falls Blvd.
North Tonawanda, NY 14120
(800) 456-3003
www.mhs.com

Neurology, Learning and Behavior Center
230 500 East, Suite 100
Salt Lake City, UT 84102
(801) 532-1484

PCI Educational Publishing
12029 Warfield
San Antonio, TX 78216
(800) 594-4263
www.pcicatalog.com

Prentice Hall/Center for Applied Research in Education
200 Old Tappan Road
Old Tappan, NJ 07675
(800) 922-0579

Slosson Educational Publications
P.O. Box 280
East Aurora, NY 14052
(888) 756-7766
www.slosson.com

Sopris West
P.O. Box 1809
Longmont, CO 80502-1809
(800) 547-6747
www.sopriswest.com

Western Psychological Services
Creative Therapy Store
12031 Wilshire Blvd.
Los Angeles, CA 90025
(800) 648-8857

Index